Kaleidoscope: Life's Meaningful Reflections

Vanessa Conaway Pace

Volume Two

One Great Gift

Pace Publishing International
Post Office Box 2187
Lynnwood, WA 98036

www.pacepublishing.com

Kaleidoscope: Life's Meaningful Reflections
Volume 2: One Great Gift

Prose, Poetry, Music, and Design Created By:

Vanessa Conaway Pace

Cover Design by: milagraphicartist@gmail.com

ISBN Number: ISBN-13: 978-0-9704373-1-0
                          ISBN-10: 0-9704373-1-5

Copyright © 2018 by: Pace Publishing
                              Post Office Box 2187
                              Lynnwood, WA 98036 USA

                              www.pacepublishing.com

Printed/Duplicated in the United States of America. All rights to this book and its design are reserved to the Author under International Copyright Law. No part of this design, these contents and/or cover may be reproduced in whole or in part in any form by any means—electronic, mechanical, photocopy, video or audio recording, or any other—except for brief quotations in printed reviews, without the prior express written consent of the Publisher.

About The Author

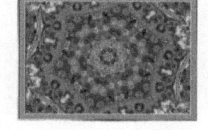

Vanessa Conaway Pace is a direct descendant of the Welsh Bards, and is an Award-Winning Poet, "with the distinction of Poet Fellow, in honor of creative work", by Nobel House, London, England, 2007. (See pages 97 and 179.) This current Volume is the second in the **"Kaleidoscope"** Books and Audio Series of **"Life's Meaningful Reflections"**.

She is an international singer with 9 albums (in 5 languages) to her credit, is Host and Producer of two long-running weekly half-hour television series, along with numerous television specials, and is a frequent presenter at conferences and seminars.

Vanessa is creator of the voice training books and audio series entitled "Managing Your Computerized Voice Box", and is Co-Author of "For The Love Of Children: A Guidebook for Early Childhood Education".

As a Teacher of the Creative Arts, Vanessa Coaches Voice in her Studio in Lynnwood, WA, and internationally via electronic media. She holds a Bachelor of Arts Degree in Music Performance, and maintains a varied performing career ranging from Opera to Broadway.

> "My Life's Kaleidoscope is ever-changing: ...:
> Writing, Singing, Teaching, Coaching, Creating, Concertizing, Producing books/greeting cards/albums, ...,
>
> "..., Learning/Researching/Lecturing about The Power of Sound and the scientific and esoteric basis thereof, ...,
>
> "What a wonderful world we have to explore, and understand, and subdue!"
> Vanessa

Other Books and Materials By This Author

Also in the **"Kaleidoscope"** Series: "Kaleidoscope: Life's Meaningful Reflections" Volume 1: "Techno" Indeed!!!

"For The Love Of Children: A Guidebook for Early Childhood Education";
with Marguerite Laskares and Tamra Pace

"Secrets of Voice Development for Speakers and Singers"
Course Numbers 1 and 2

"Rejoice! A Celebration of Christmas" Music Cd

"He's Alive!!!": Gospel Music Cd, Sung in English

"El E Viu": Gospel Music Cd, Sung in Romanian

"Yazutse!!!: Gospel Music Cd, Sung in Kenyarwandan
(the native language of Rwanda)

"The Master's Voice": Hymns in Classical Settings,
Sung in English

"Lodiamo Dio": Hymns in Classical Settings,
Sung in Italian

"Din Dragostea": "To Romania With Love",
Hymns in Classical Settings, Sung in Romanian

"Great Classical Arias and Duets":
with Finnish Coloratura Mezzo Soprano
Helena Niemispelto;
Sung in English, Italian, Finnish, and Latin
www.pacepublishing.com

Dedication

*To Mother and Daddy,
Freeda and George Conaway,
who gave me a love for words,
and their meaning,
and their power,
and their expressive beauty.*

*Thanks for all those hours
when you read to me,
and encouraged me,
and helped me
to Be Who I AM!*

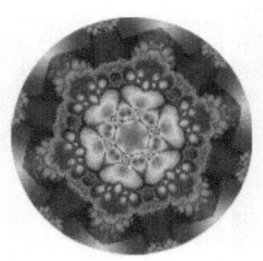

www.pacepublishing.com

Acknowledgements

Many a Seeker
    Has gone on before
        And left us
            Some Truths
              So We
                  Could learn more.

They've toiled,
    And They've pondered,
        And thought,
            And cajoled,
                To gather
                    The Secrets
                        From the Masters
                          Of old.

They've wrangled,
    And struggled,
        And reasoned,
            And read,
                Until They
                    Had so many thoughts
                        In Their head,

That They saw
    A great picture
        Of how things transpire,
            And they got it
                By blood, sweat, and tears,...,
                ..., Not by hire!

They discovered,
    And studied,
        And thought
            Those things through,
                And even "Remembered"
                    Old Stuff
                        That They knew.

They suffered the hardships
    Of lessons
        Well learned,
            And worked with
                The facts
                    And the figures
                        They'd churned,

And stretched
    Themselves out
        Just as far
            As They could,
                With the fervor
                    That only
                      A pioneer
                          Would.

But it takes
    So much more
        Than hard work
            And toil;...;
                It takes
                    Open hearts, ...,
                        Open minds,...,
                          ..., Fertile soil,

In which
> *Seeds of Greatness*
>> *Can sprout up*
>>> *And grow,*
>>>> *And be trusted*
>>>>> *With Truths*
>>>>>> *That some others*
>>>>>>> *Must know.*

And We,
> *Who are searching*
>> *For answers,*
>>> *And news,*
>>>> *Can glean*
>>>>> *From Their works*
>>>>>> *Some great Truths*
>>>>>>> *We can use*

In our journey
> *From Neophyte*
>> *Here in this Earth,*
>>> *To a Sage*
>>>> *Who's produced*
>>>>> *Higher thoughts*
>>>>>> *Of great worth,*

That will, in turn,
> *Benefit others*
>> *Who follow,*
>>> *So their lives*
>>>> *And their minds*
>>>>> *Will not be*
>>>>>> *So hollow!*

A big "**thanks**"
    To the faithful,
        Who have
            Paid the price,
                So We
                    Can do likewise
                        With our turn
                            At the dice!

You've made
    Our lives better
        By your great
            Successes,
                And left us
                    Some tools
                        To help us
                            Avoid messes;

And You've added Your share
    To Earth's
        Burgeoning Treasure
            Of Wisdom,
                And Knowledge,
                    And Joy
                        Without measure!

So that We
    Can now study
        Your great work
            In stages,
                Which will help us
                    Throw Light
                        On the dusty
                            Dark Ages!

We acknowledge
    Your Libraries,
        Tools, and inventions,
            And honor
                Your faithfulness,
                    Thoughts,
                        And intentions.

Now, May We
    Be worthy
        To take what You've done,
            And add on
                Our piece
                    That We've gleaned
                        On this run.

And help other
    Interested parties
        Return
            To the awareness
                That We're each
                    A Heavenly Intern!

Who, together,
    Pass on
        To those who shall come,
            The Keys To The Kingdom,
        That We
            Have come from!!!

Yes!!! We're Seeker's,
    And Senders,
        And Mender's
           Of LIGHT,
                And we gratefully
                    Acknowledge,
                    To us,
YOU"RE OUTTA SIGHT!!!

                        Vanessa Conaway Pace
            February 11, 2015, Lynnwood, Washington

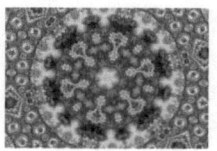

My deep gratitude also goes to my friend and colleague,
Marguerite Laskares, who has taken time from her own
brilliant work in Early Childhood Education*,
to provide invaluable editorial and production
assistance on this Volume.

Many thanks for all those happy creative hours!!!

*See "For The Love Of Children: A Guidebook For Early Childhood",
Marguerite Laskares at Amazon.com.

*"**Kaleidoscope,** n. 1. an optical tube in which bits of glass and beads are shown in changing symmetrical forms by reflection in two or more mirrors as the tube is turned. 2. anything that shifts continually."*
The Random House Dictionary,
Ballentine Books, New York

*"**Kaleidoscope** , ...; picturesquely diversified."*
The Practical Standard Dictionary
of the English Language,
Funk & Wagnalls Company,
New York, *1928*

www.pacepublishing.com

Table of Contents

Frontispieces

About the Author	3
Other Books and Publications by the Author	4
Dedication	5
Acknowledgements	7
Prologue	17
Foreword	21
Epigraph	25
Introduction	27

Reflections

There Is Something To Sing About!!!	37
Inspirational Background	39
Poem	43
Song	47
Reader's Reflections	51
I AM Creator	57
Inspirational Background	59
Poem	63
Reader's Reflections	69
Where Am I?	75
Inspirational Background	77
Poem	83
Reader's Reflections	91
<u>That's</u> A Lot of Rot!!!	97
Inspirational Background	99
Poem	109
Song	117
Reader's Reflections	129

Sound The Trumpet ... 135
    Inspirational Background ... 137
    Poem ... 147
    Reader's Reflections ... 155

Am I ??? ... 161
    Inspirational Background ... 163
    Poem ... 169
    Reader's Reflections ... 173

Green Seasons ... 179
    Inspirational Background ... 181
    Poem ... 191
    Reader's Reflections ... 195

Light ... 203
    Inspirational Background ... 205
    Poem ... 213
    Reader's Reflections ... 217

One Great Gift ... 223
    Inspirational Background ... 225
    Poem ... 233
    Song ... 239
    Reader's Reflections ... 245

Epilogue ... 251
    Poem ... 253
    Reader's Reflections ... 259

Reading List ... 265

Prologue

www.pacepublishing.com

Dear Seeker of Those **"Deeper Things"**,

    Come share a cup
        Of tea with me
            As we share
                Thoughts in Poetry.

    Pull up a chair,
        A cot, or bed,
            And ponder Words
                That you have read.

    Allow new thoughts
        To filter through, ...,
            They'll lead you
                To a path that's "new".

    The old "me"
        Now has given way
            To paths We walk
                This current day;

    So now, We need
        A fresher look, ...,
            New views will surface
                Through this book!

    We'll find that,
        If We open up,
            We'll have new food
                And drink to sup;

    And Life will find
        New Songs to Sing,
            With a Poet who's Loving
                This Earth-time Fling!!!

                        Vanessa

www.pacepublishing.com

Foreword

The soul
      Of the Poet
           Asks questions
                And ponders
                      On what
                          Things might **mean**

           If We thought
               With some different
                   Behestions
                       With a Mind
                           That is calm
                              And serene.

The angles
      From which
           Our perspective
                Has been guided
                     For so many years

      Have been formed
           By a numbing
                Invective
                     That has steered
                        Our advance
                           To the rears!

But the time
　　Has now come
　　　　For the masses
　　　　　　To wonder
　　　　　　　　How things
　　　　　　　　　　Came to be
　　　　　　And to help
　　　　　　　　Lift us out
　　　　　　　　　　Of morasses
　　　　　　　　　　　　So that We
　　　　　　　　　　　　　　Can all live
　　　　　　　　　　　　　　　　Comf'tably

On an Earth
　　That is teeming
　　　　With Life Forms
　　　　　　That are healthy
　　　　　　　　And happy to be
　　　　　　In a rarefied air
　　　　　　　　That supports them all there
　　　　　　　　　　To the absolute Top
　　　　　　　　　　　　N'th degree.

Where The Laws
　　Of Creation
　　　　Will guide them
　　　　　　Into lives
　　　　　　　　Of compassion
　　　　　　　　　　And Love,
　　　　　　As We lived long before
　　　　　　　　In those great days
　　　　　　　　　　Of yore
　　　　　　　　In that Home
　　　　　　　　　　Which We're now
　　　　　　　　　　　　Dreaming of.

But **The Poet**
    Can help us all
        Get there
            By encouraging
                Us all
                    To THINK,
        And to welcome Us all
            With a clarion call
                That can bring us all back
                    From the brink

So, this Poet
    Is sharing
        Some thoughts here
            In the hope
                That some others will, too,
        And together we'll brave
            This new frontier
                With the heart
                    Of the poet's purview;

For the musings
    Of these Ones
        Are poetic
            And imagined,
                And soulful
                    And warm,
And they're wrestled, and bought,
    By reflection
        And thought,
            And imparted
                By word-painted Form.

                    Vanessa Conaway Pace
        Lynnwood, Washington, February 21, 2015

Welcome to my world!!!

www.pacepublishing.com

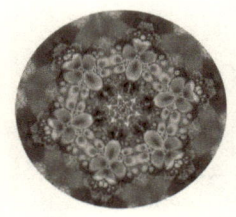

"cre-ate´, ..., 1. To cause to come into existence; especially, to produce out of nothing. 2. To produce as a new construction out of existing materials."

The Practical Standard Dictionary;
Funk & Wagnalls Company,
New York, 1928

Oh, I feel a poem coming on!!! ....

"cre-a´tion, ..., 1. The act of creating;
production without use of preexistent material;
...; 2. An act of construction,
physical or mental;
the combining or organizing
of existing materials
into new form; ...."

> The Practical Standard Dictionary;
> Funk & Wagnalls Company,
> New York, 1928

Oh, I do, indeed, feel poems coming on!!!
...

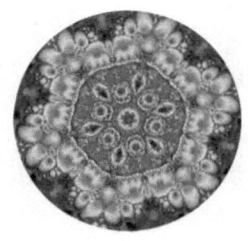

Introduction

Must Read!!!

> "Whoso is industrious
> shall also succeed."
> Johann Sebastian Bach
> (March 31, 1685-July 28, 1750)

I love the music of Bach (German composer and organist, who is widely regarded as one of the greatest composers of all time). It deepens the soul and organizes the mind like no other music. And to call him a **prolific** composer of great music would be a colossal understatement! The volumes and volumes of music that he produced and performed during his lifetime are enough to make any composer (or **any creative person**, for that matter) take up the tools of the creative endeavor that gives them great joy, and get "industrious"!

Bach believed that he must work hard, and the fruits of his labors have been highly sought after, played, and enjoyed for centuries. Other musicians have spent lifetimes studying the works of the Master (one notable *example is the brilliant concert pianist Glenn Gould), using his legacy to deepen their own skills and enlighten others with his high level of musical excellence.*

Music history tells us that he developed some of his works as methodologies with which he trained the 210 members of his progeny in their own pursuits of music. Others he created as performance pieces for the local singers and orchestras of his day to use in spiritual celebrations and entertainments.

*Yes, Bach certainly proved his belief that one must be industrious in order to succeed. But let's look at another reason for his success. Perhaps he was successful, not because he did a lot of hours of work, and was always busy at it, but I submit that his success may have really been because of his **passion** for the field in which he was successful. He **loved** music. He was gifted in music. He was born into a whole family who loved music. He came to this planet with an assignment, a contract, an agreement to use the gifts and talents that were within him to create beauty for the planet and enlightenment in the people. And it worked!*

If we look around in our society, and maybe even in ourselves, today we can observe that we have many people who are working very hard. They are putting in long hours, faithfully showing up for jobs that admittedly give them no real joy, and that oftentimes do not even use the gifts and talents that are secretly buried deep inside, and are slavishly doing busy work that takes up their time and energy, and all in the mistaken belief that that is the only way they can pay the bills. But, wait! Maybe there is another way! Maybe the "Bach's" of this world have actually paid the bills by doing what they loved and were equipped to do! Maybe there's a way for us to pay the bills by doing what we really love to do!

Marsha Sinetar wrote a wonderful book entitled "Do What You Love, The Money Will Follow: Discovering Your Right Livelihood", and it was a great inspiration to my life. It came into my hands, as books often do, just at the time when I needed a little more encouragement to go on with my sure knowing that I could no longer go on with the charade that I was living. For 25 years I dutifully went to "the job", faithfully *performing my duties, but all the while withering up inside because of a lack of time and energy to pursue the real joy of my life, or should I say **joys** of my life, which were singing, writing, and nurturing my wonderful family, all of which I was forced to do with leftover energy after I had worked all day to build someone else's kingdom. The paycheck wasn't all that great! Yes, it got us through, but there came a day when I simply had to try. I had to allow myself at least the opportunity to do what I love to do as the first priority in my life, not on the leftovers.*

I had had a good example. My parents had taken the plunge, and had left the security of "good", but controlling, jobs, and in true pioneering spirit, had bought a farm in order to be free to follow their own path and build a life where they could follow their passions, develop their interests and talents, and still have time to sit on the porch in the evening and sing, or tell stories, or simply listen to the crickets and the frogs chirping happily in the cool mountain air, and watch the stars as they marched across a sky that was dark enough that those beautiful celestial lights were visible.

They did it, they made it, and we had a wonderful life. In the process of doing what they wanted to do they not only supported us financially, but they had the time and the energy to nurture and grow two children to the point that we were strong enough, well-educated enough, and self-confident enough that we could take the same steps for our own lives. We didn't have a lot of money, but they bought everything for cash. We didn't have a new car until they could walk into the dealership and plop down the cash for it. I remember the day. I remember the sense of self satisfaction. WE did it with our own hands, and they owed no man anything.

They were loved and respected by all. They were trusted by all. And they treated others in like manner. Like Johann Sebastian Bach, they were "industrious". Often we were all tired, but they slept well, breathed deeply, and walked in the peace of knowing that they were their own person. A life in that state is free to create all that you can imagine to do.

After I acted in that seemingly brash manner, quit my secure daytime job, and threw myself full force into the pursuit of my dreams, I had many opportunities to rethink what some would call "my folly". It was not always easy, but it has been quite a ride! I wouldn't trade any of it. .... No! Not for a moment.

But there were "moments". "How will I pay the bills this month?" "How will I feed the family today?" "How will I put gas in the tank to get to the next singing job?" But I made it! Like my parents before me, I made it! I learned to be used to living in what some would call "miracles", and I even learned to expect them. It's a lesson I could never have learned in the "security" of my daytime job. I learned that there are different and higher ways that provision can come to us. I learned that just setting my intention out there to accomplish some goal that was important to me would somehow bring the provision to make it happen.

That's not always a comfortable way of life! But the more we practice the skills of living on the edge, the more we understand that we are not alone, that there are unseen forces that are assigned to ensure our success, and that the excitement of triumphing in adversity is really what draws many people into the competitions of the Olympic Games, and millions of people to watch! It sure beats the doldrums of the 9 to 5 routine. And in the process, we develop the gifts and talents within us, the emotional strengths necessary for our spiritual, emotional, and intellectual advancement, and the satisfactions of a life well lived.

Yes, Johann Sebastian Bach is right in his admonition to work hard and to be "industrious". But to work hard in the pursuit of being something that we are not, seems to me to be a perfect definition of "futility". We just end up tired, depressed, bitter, and defeated. But to work diligently on the **passion** of our lives, doing the every day disciplines that the development of anything worthwhile requires, having the courage to take the risks of sharing it with others, and believing in ourselves enough to do it over, and over, and over again adds a real spice to our lives!

And, yes, the choices that we make to follow our dreams, and to make of ourselves **everything that we possibly can be**, are important, nay, life giving to ourselves. And, there is another dimension to this also. Others are watching. Others are looking for encouragement to dare to become all that **they** can be. We all know how difficult it is to stick our heads above the crowd, and dare to be different, when we are alone. But when others see us doing it, then they are encouraged to do it also. And then, when two of us do it, we can attract a crowd! Yes! Others are watching. Children learn it from the example of their parents. Friends learn from the example of their peers. And we all have had the examples of others who have gone before us, and whose shoulders we can stand on if we will take the time to learn from their stories and accomplishments. Their stories have been written and passed down for our enlightenment. We gain strength from their successes, knowledge from their endeavors, and can then carry on their great traditions, like those that were passed down to us by Johann Sebastian Bach. When we dare to draw on the resources that were innate in us when we landed on this planet, and we courageously follow the Path that was planned for us for this trip, and we faithfully do the work with a wholehearted endeavor, we shall surely have a successful life, as promised in Mr. Bach's quote above, and shall lay a sufficient foundation for a more advanced life the next time around!

So, the first step is to do the internal work of honestly answering the questions, "What am I truly passionate about?" "What is that unique interest that I have, and that I am willing to devote the energies of my life to pursuing?" (In other words, "Who is the Real Me?", and, "Why am I here at this time?"),..., What am I uniquely equipped to do?", and, "Is there anybody out there who will help me to do it?"!!!

Go ahead. I dare you! Find out who you REALLY are! Grapple with those questions until you come up with something that makes sense to you, and then go after it with all your heart, soul, mind, and might. You're the only one who can do it for you, and there will be a whole universe full of people who will join you in the celebrations!

Oh! I really do feel **a bunch** of poems coming on!!!

www.pacepublishing.com

There Is Something To Sing About!!!

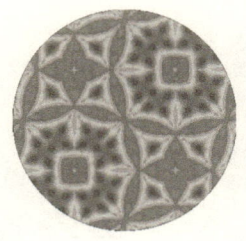

www.pacepublishing.com

"There Is Something To Sing About"
Inspirational Background

Why Sing? Why should we go to all the effort to open our own mouths, breathe deeply, and freely express our own thoughts and feelings with our own voice, thus making ourselves open and vulnerable to the opinions and criticisms of others?

In this is age of personal electronic devices, and personal earplugs, and protected personal spaces, it has somehow become taboo to actually fill up the air around us with our own vocal projections of ourselves! We might disturb somebody, ..., Some thing, ... Music has become for many something that lives only in our ear buds, or streaming through the television screen, while We feel empty, stifled, and shut down, ..., required to allow ourselves to be pummeled by the sounds of "the professionals", and the noises of our industrialized society around us.

But, what about singing in your own song? What about humming contentedly while you work, or gleefully *expressing your delight, like children on the playground of life, or, confidently using your on-board musical instrument as a creative tool to Sing creative projects and ideas into existence? Stories in the ancient literature described such creative events, so why should they be the only ones having such fun? They were simply putting the known laws of physics, sound, and music into practice, and getting the expected results. When We use the universal laws of creation there is no limit to what We can achieve. Since science is now confirming to us what the Ancients have known from antiquity, that everything is made of music, then it's time for us here-tofore Earth-bound Hu-mans to wake up to the empowering fact that Singing is a powerful expressive and creative force,* **and we all came equipped to do it!**

If we think about it, Singing is a natural and powerful way that we can get our thoughts and emotions up and out of our bodies. By simply opening our mouth and throat, and catapulting our sounds out by a simple upward flip of our diaphragm We can send forth the energy waves that we produce when we think, emote, and sing. Those vibrations that we send out are extensions of ourselves, and they create the surroundings in which we live.

Wow! That means we are actually in control after all!! No more being a "victim" of someone else's rule over our life. We can change the song of our thoughts and emotions, and that will change our lives!

Try it! You will find the results amazing! The next time you are tempted to succumb to a full-blown pity party, start creating a new atmosphere around you. Sing a happy song that you remember hearing, or, just begin to use your voice to express your feelings. Sing in words, or syllables, or moans, but don't stop singing until you have released all the sadness and the stress that invited you to the pity party. Then begin to sing a new song of hope, gratitude, joy, and gladness.

Begin to Sing over things as you would like them to be. Out with the old, and in with the new! Sing out words, intentions, and tones to create the New World of Beauty, Love, and Light that We are all longing to see. Then, as You send out those "vibes", since like attracts like, they will join with the songs of other like-minded Ones, and together We will create the world We want to see!

Oh, double **Wow!** It's all in our hands, and We have everything we need to do it right there in our Hearts, Minds, and Throats!

Now **THAT's** worth Singing about!

Oh, I do feel a poem coming on, and my Voice wants to **Sing** it!!!

Poem
There Is Something To Sing About!!!

There is something **within You**
That longs to give Praise
So lift up **Your Voice**
To the "**Ancient of Days**"
And **Sing** from within
Of Our Glorious Home

And tell of its wonders
Wherever You roam!

CHORUS
Oh, there's something to **Sing** about!!! ...,
Something to **Shout!!!** ...,
So open **Your Voice** ...
And let Your Glory come out!!!
And **Sing** and **Rejoice**
For the work that's been done
In that Wondrous "**Creation**"
With which We are ONE!!!

Its **THAT Life** that's within You;

That **knows how to Sing**!!!!!

And rises in Praise;

Let the Angel**US** **RING**!!!!!!!!

That Life **wants** to shout, **"Glory!"**

From each mountain top

And **Sing** out in Praises

That **never will stop!**

CHORUS

Oh, there's something to **Sing** about!!! ...,

Something to **Shout!!!** ...,

So open **Your Voice** ...,

And let Your Glory come out!!!

And **Sing** and **Rejoice**

For the work that's been done

In that Wondrous **"Creation"**

With which We are ONE!!!

For the mountains **Sing** *praise*

And the trees clap their hands

With the stars of the heavens

And numberless sands

As the created Universe

Rises to **Sing**

Let **Us,**

"The Creation"

Now join in and **Sing!**

CHORUS

Oh, there's something to **Sing** *about!!! ...,*

Something to **Shout!!! ...,**

So open **Your Voice** *...,*

And let Your Glory come out!!!

And **Sing** *and* **Rejoice**

For the work that's been done

In that Wondrous **"Creation"**

With which We are ONE!!!

Through the ages and ages
Eternity rolls;
And may it be filled
With the **Songs of Our Souls**
Breathing praise from Our Spirits
We join in and **Sing**

Of the **matchless "Creation"**
O'er which
We are **King!!!!**

CHORUS

Oh, there's something to **Sing** about!!! ...,
Something to **Shout!!!** ...,
So open **Your Voice** ...,
And let Your Glory come out!!!
And **Sing** and **Rejoice**
For the work that's been done
In that Wondrous **"Creation"**
With which We are ONE!!!

© 2005 *Vanessa Conaway Pace*
Seattle, Washington, September 30, 2005

Song

There Is Something To Sing About!!!

Vanessa Conaway Pace   Vanessa Conaway Pace

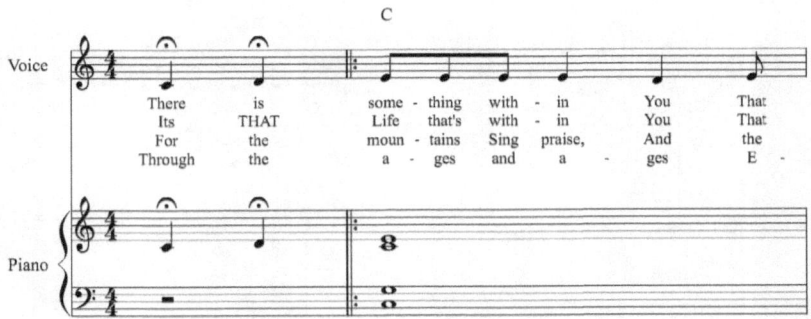

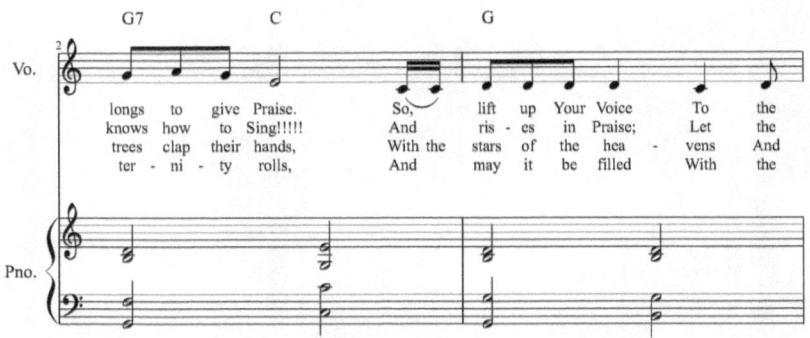

September 30, 2005

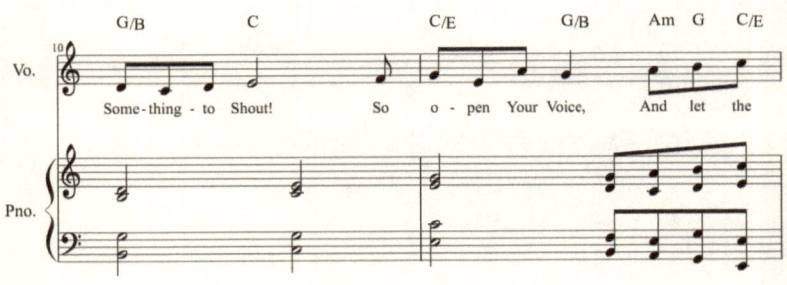

There Is Something To Sing About!!!

This Is Your
Invitation
To Create!

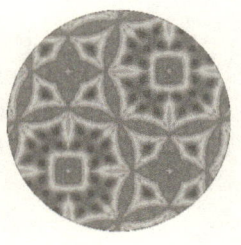

Dear Seeker of Those "Deeper Things",

There **IS** Something within You
    That longs to give praise,
        So take up your tools
            And enlighten Our haze
    With Your ideas
        And creations
            In the form
                That You choose;
        Go ahead! ...!
            Do it now! ...!
                Do not let
                    Your Muse
                        Snooze!

Let Your
    Creative flow
        Trickle down
            To the Sea
                Of Great Beauty
                    That feeds
                        Our Great
                            Humanity.

Yes! There is room in the ocean
    For the waters you bring
        From the core of your being, ...,
            Your creative Wellspring; ...;

        So lower your bucket
            Then pull up the rope,
                And **create** the things
                    That you planned
                        With great Hope!

Now Its YOUR Turn To Be "Creator"!
Put YOUR Thoughts Here, and Read Them Later!

Take out a pencil,
    A pen,
        And some paper,
            And put down
                Some Plans
                    For Your
                        Creative Caper!

*Now Its YOUR Turn To Be "Creator"!
Put YOUR Thoughts Here, and Read Them Later!*

Now Its YOUR Turn To Be "Creator"!
Put YOUR Thoughts Here, and Read Them Later!

Now Its YOUR Turn To Be "Creator"!
Put YOUR Thoughts Here, and Read Them Later!

I AM Creator

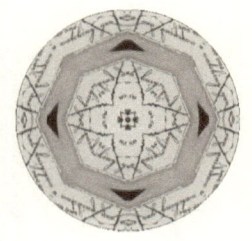

www.pacepublishing.com

"I AM Creator"
Inspirational Background

There was a question, …, No, **two** questions, that kept rolling around in what we'll call "my mind" (until we get a better location), and it was getting harder and harder to ignore them. But each time they surfaced I'd cleverly tuck them back in the tickler file to wait for a more opportune moment.

After all, I had important things to think about that consumed my time and energies, …, like what I'd sing in the next concert; or, what I would get the children for Christmas (and how I'd pay for it!); or, how I would manage to fill the gas tank for the next week's activities; and, most urgently, how I could possibly balance long work hours, the ever-present chores to keep my home humming, the Herculean effort of keeping my family together, the demands of building my career, university classes that required massive hours of attendance and preparation, and the inviolable schedule of Voice Coaching Sessions with my Beloved Maestro Silvio Coscia; etc., etc., etc. Life already had its challenges, and physical, mental, and emotional demands. The water in my well seemed to be a long way from the surface, and the rope on my bucket seemed to be getting shorter and shorter by the day. Nope! No time to ponder anything that does not directly relate to service, sacrifice, survival, and singing!

But, faintly, in the background, the song played on: "Who AM I?" And "Why AM I here?" It is our good fortune, and a tribute to our spiritual heritage, that Something within us is ever drawing us Home, and through the years this gentle, but incessantly nudging need-to-know simmered on the back burner. Every once in a while I'd open the lid and stir it, but,..., ..., Gotta go! ..., There is yet another important deadline to meet;...; Yet another crisis that would extract huge amounts from my physical, mental, and emotional bank accounts. These challenges were not the kind that stretches one's loftier pursuits (although I thought they were at the time), but rather, seemed to be limited to coping skills and problem solving, with no room for exploring the Great Truths, or the actual meaning of Life. No time or energy to think on that. And, on the surface, there was no inclination to think on things like that. I had my church. I had my education. And they had already answered all of those questions. Mine but to learn their teachings, and obey:

Mine not to reason why,
    But just to watch my life go by,
        Working for the other guy,
            While all my dreams are on standby.

But one day I experienced another one of those "Thanks! I needed that", slaps in the face when I was doing some late-night surfing on the Internet, and caught a glimpse of a three-level depiction of the "I Am Presence". Something felt very familiar. There were three levels of Beings: The one on the bottom was in the form of a Human Being that looked like me. The middle Being directly above "me" was obviously much more evolved than the "me" in the lower level, and glowed with the golden-orbed Presence that we would recognize as an "Angel" or a much higher evolved Being with gossamer robes and a circle of golden light indicating high levels of enlightenment. And then, the third level was perfectly balanced emanations of Glorious Light, reflecting the ineffable Glories of the Source of all Life! And, they were all three connected by a Ray of Light descending through the head and heart.

All of a sudden I understood that my "angel that always beholds the face of God" was really what was being depicted on the top level of the drawing! And, if I, the boots-on-the-ground individualized Presence of God that drives around this planet in an earth-suit we call a body, were the bottom level of that picture, then that middle person would have to be my Higher Self! It all made perfect sense! I immediately recognized this three-part Being as a depiction of the Real Me, My I AM Presence, with all my potential to Be Who I really AM!

Now, if "I" (the ground-level Being) could master my thoughts, emotions, needs, and intentions, and bring them up to the loftier level that my Higher Self (the middle-level Being) lives on, then my middle level "Friend that sticks closer than a brother" would also help me to fulfill my purpose here, and it would surely help me to ascend to the even higher-level of Being that watches over both of us from the higher level of the diagram. And, I could eventually ascend back up to the even higher Love heights from which I chose to come! And, since all three parts of my three-part Being were connected through the Heart, then We would All be One once again!!!

Oh! **Wow!** That is definitely something to Sing about!!! I do in indeed feel a poem coming on!

Poem
I AM Creator

I AM **Creator**, *and,*
    I AM **Divine**, *and,*
        I AM **attached**
            To **The I AM VINE!**

I AM **The Life**, *and,*
    I AM **The Breath**, *and,*
        I AM **The Conqueror**,
            Even over death.

I AM **The Love**, *and,*
    I AM **complete**, *and,*
        I AM **a part**
            Of **Perfection's ELITE!!!**

That I AM's All Knowing,
And **Wisdom** Sublime
That is **Mine**
As **I** walk
The dimension
Of Time!

A Dimension that's waning
And growing more dim,
As our Earth-ship
Is sailing
Over Time's nearing rim.

When The **I AM** within us
Will begin to enforce
All the Plans
And Assignments
We've **designed** for this Course!

For We wanted to treck
This dimension of Time
For the lessons We'd learn, ...,
...We'd become
More **Sublime**; ...;

But, We also would come
    To conjoin with that Power
        That is needed
            As Earth
                Comes to **Glorious Power**.

For We all are connected
    And are part of **The Vine**
        That We've tapped in. ….
        …. ….**We c h a n n e l**
            The **Life** in that **Line**!!!

We are part of the Grid
    That is fueling this Earth;
        And We're pouring in **Life**
            As She's giving
                New Birth. …

That is giving **New** Life
    Wild, …
        … **Joyous**, …
            and **Free**
    That is healing all wounds
        To the Real You and Me! …

That is waking all Living
> With **Love**...
>> That's **Divine**;
>>> That has overcome Death,
>>>> And the shackles of Time!

Yes!!!!!!!!

    I AM **Creator**, and

    I AM **Divine**, and

    I AM attached
>> To The I AM **VINE**!!!

    I AM **The Life**, and

    I AM **The Breath**, and

    I AM **The Conqueror**,
>> Even over death.

I AM **The Love**, and

I AM **Complete**, and

I AM *a part*

Of Perfection's **ELITE***!!!

© 2005 Vanessa Conaway Pace
Seattle, Washington, April, 2005

*"Elite, n. The Choicest part, especially of a society, army, etc.; the pick; flower."

www.pacepublishing.com

I AM Creator

This Is Your *Invitation To Create!*

Dear Seeker of Those "Deeper Things",

Start thinking of how
    You're connected
        To "Source",
            And then,
                Just tap in
                    To the "Force"
                        Of that "Source".

Then, just open
    The faucet
        And let
            That flow go,
                And soon
                    You will find
                        There is a real need
                            To row!

'Cause the current
    Is taking you
        Faster and faster
            In to worlds
                That You've wanted
                    To study
                        And Master;

Where You'll find
    The great joy
        And the deep
            Satisfaction
                Of One
                    Who has taken
                      His dreams
                          Into action!

Now Its YOUR Turn To Be "Creator"!
Put YOUR Thoughts Here, and Read Them Later!

Now,
    Take out Your Book
        And scratch out
           Your Plan
              And then,
                  Execute it
                      As fast
                          As You can!

*Now Its YOUR Turn To Be "Creator"!
Put YOUR Thoughts Here, and Read Them Later!*

Now Its YOUR Turn To Be "Creator"!
Put YOUR Thoughts Here, and Read Them Later!

Now Its YOUR Turn To Be "Creator"!
Put YOUR Thoughts Here, and Read Them Later!

Where Am I?

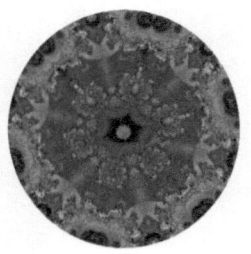

www.pacepublishing.com

"Where Am I?"
Inspirational Background

> "We cannot solve our problems with the same thinking we used when we created them."
>
> Albert Einstein

*Life. ..., **My** life. .... **Our** life. .... **Planet Earth's** life. .... **The Universe's** life. ....* Is it all inexorably tumbling toward a future that is cast in stone, or, can I/We change it? And, if I/We can change it, then **how**? Is there anything I/We can do, think, or say that can alter the course of life, or, do I/We simply have to play with the cards I/We have been dealt, and hope for the best?

It is a bit overwhelming to ponder on the infinite possibilities that "life" has to offer us, ..., especially when one has spent a number of years thinking that all there is to life is what our five senses allow us to experience, or, what our clever minds can dream up, or what some outside entity has deigned to bestow upon its subjects, ..., to suddenly awaken to the interesting possibility that there may be more to the "Real Me" than meets the eye.

All along I had been taught that my "success" in life was dependent upon my ambition, training, and *preparation, the thoughts my clever mind could conjure up, and the luck of the draw in the experiences that life handed me. But, could it be that who and where we are in life is determined by the way we look at the events of life, and how we respond to (or, take charge of) them? Hmmmm! And, if I can change them, and, if Mr. Einstein is right, then there must be something inside of me that is connected to something that is more than Earthbound "Me", that can make something higher than my current existence come into being.* **Wow! That's worth pondering!**

Peggy Lee's 1969 song droned the question, "Is That All There Is?", and then seemingly wearily resigns itself to the bleakness of it all with, "If that's all there is to life then let's keep dancing." And then, low point of the low points, moans, "Let's break out the booze and have a ball, if that's all there is".

The writers of that song, Jerry Leiver and Mike Stoller, may have had that depressive outlook on life, but no one knows for sure, because the lyrics were so deftly written and wonderfully ambiguous that they become a mirror that each listener sees his own truth in. And, like the enigmatic Mona Lisa, from what I can read, they never let the cat out of the bag either way! However, it is said that Peggy Lee's wonderfully expressive voice (and intention?) may have portrayed a different picture.

The song intersperses spoken narratives of traumatic events in life (lost possessions, lost lovers, high ecstasies, and even the expected disappointment of death) with what seems to be the dull and languishing mantra, "Is that all there is? ...". IF we were to accept the "downer" interpretation of the song, then we would have to cry with the Epicureans of old, "Eat, drink, and be merry, for tomorrow we may die". But, maybe there is another interpretation. (History tells us that the Epicurean philosophy held, among other things, that the goal of human life is happiness, characterized by the absence of pain and mental strife. Was there something wrong with that thinking??!!!)

Maybe it's really an "upper". One analysis of the lyrics could be that it is obviously the song of a person who has felt great pain, had faced that pain, and, therefore, could also feel great pleasure. They had also experienced the touted ecstasies of life, and realized that they were just that,..., another experience. Perhaps the real message for

Peggy was that neither emotional extreme could destroy her. The record shows that the personal experiences of Peggy Lee's life may have been mirrored in the words of the song, but she sang them with a happy quality in her voice that subtly said, "It'll take more than that to destroy me!" Is there a valuable lesson here for us all?

Peggy Lee (May 26, 1920 – January 21, 2002) was an American jazz and popular music singer, songwriter, composer, and a gifted actress who could inhabit the lyrics of the song. She lived it, and then carried that acting talent into the real-life circumstances of everyday life. She was perceived by her audiences to be down to the bones realistic, and her adoring fans loved her for it. Yes, maybe there is a valuable lesson for us all to learn here. Facing life sensitively and honestly is a giant step toward emotional health!

The famous actor James Cagney gave this wonderful advice about acting, "Stand still, look the audience or the co-player in the eye, and tell 'em the truth." Real acting is telling the truth, and so it must be in real life.

Another famous James Cagney quote is, "There's not much to say about acting but this. Never settle back on your heels. Never relax. If you relax, the audience relaxes. And always mean everything you say." Again, the art of acting teaches us some real life secrets to a successful life!

"**All the world's a stage**" is the phrase that begins a monologue from Act II, Scene VII of William Shakespeare's "As You Like It", spoken by the melancholy Jaques. The speech compares the world to a stage, and life to a play, and catalogues the seven stages of a man's life, (sometimes referred to as the **seven ages of man**): infant, schoolboy, lover, soldier, justice, Pantalone, and old age.

If William Shakespeare was right, and who would dare to disagree with such a genius, then maybe we can take a lesson from both the Poet Supreme himself and from Peggy Lee's song. Jaques' famous quote in Act II Scene VII of "As You Like It" declares that,

> "All the world's a stage, and all the men and women merely players: they have their exits and their entrances; and one man in his time plays many parts, his acts being seven ages.".

If truly we are all actors on the stage of life, then when the script of the drama of our lives gets turbulent, emotional, or even pleasantly eventful, we can disconnectedly act the part, receive the applause, and then, afterward go home to the "Real Me" that lives inside, and know that the "Real Me" is not limited to the drama of the script!

There are stories of actors and actresses who have so become the character they are playing that they can no longer separate the two identities. Disaster will always follow when a person allows him/herself to become what the core of their Being is not. The "Real Me" lives safely and calmly on the inside, and will still be peacefully and triumphantly living there long after the outside drama is over!!!

Who, and where we are is determined by the way we choose to look at the external dramas of life. And the way we choose to look at them is determined by the inner connection that we have to the Source of the "Real Me" that is safely ensconced within our Heart of Hearts.

Ahhhh! Victim no more! I get to write my own scripts, and choose my own responses to life's dramas!

Now **that's** worth rhyming about! .... My settled heart feels a poem coming on!

Poem
Where Am I?

Am I within the Being
    Of my One True Heart?

        Am I the One I was,
        And knew,
            Right from the start?

Am I the One who **Talks**
    And **Laughs**,
    And **Loves**,
      And **Writes**,
        And **Sings???!!!!**

Or, Am I part
    Of **All That Is**, ...
        ... Including **Cosmic things???**

Am I **The Voice**
    I hear inside,
        That tells me **Truths** galore?

    Or, Am I just
        The One Who shops,
            And fills the family's store?

Am I the One
    Who longs for Peace
        At last to be restored?

    Or, Am I just
        The One Who works
            To keep from being bored?

Am I the One
    Who understands
        Great things of every kind?

    Or, Am I just
        A poor lost soul
            That's limited to **Mind**?

So, how Am *I* to know it?
    Or, can *I* truly find
        Just where *I* Am? ……..

Oh…….No!!!!!! …..
    I **might** find
        I Am …… **The I AM kind!!!!**

Am *I* to think
    That *I* might be
        A part of distant stars?

    Or, maybe that
        I could have really
            Landed here from Mars??!!

Am *I* in isolation here
    From everyone
        But Me?

    Or, Am *I* joined to others,…
        Both the Earthbound,
            And the free???

Am *I* my brother's keeper
    Whether near to me
        Or far?

    Or, Am *I* part of those
        Who do not seem to be
            On par?

You mean *I* Am
    A part of "**them**", ...,
        The ones who bring disgust?

    Oh, You CAN'T mean
        That We're ALL ONE!!! ...
            THAT really IS a "**Bust**"!!!!

And here, I thought
    That We could look askance
        At "**them**"; Oh, Woe! .....

    For now I find
        That We, **as gods,**
        Must throw
            Light on their show!!!!

Since We are One
> With All That Is
>> And All That Is is ONE
>>> If I don't help my brother out
>>>> Then **WE**
>>>>> Will be UNDONE!

And maybe
> He won't CHOOSE to come
>> From darkness into Light.

>> Its still OKAY
>>> **Because my Love**
>>>> **Allows** him to be right.

I'll hold that Love
> Within my Heart
>> Until We two are **One;**

>> Until We **Both** can realize
>>> **We've** come out
>>>> **From beyond The SUN!!!!**

For **We** were never really
>Separated
>>*From* **That SOURCE;**

>>>We simply **Both** agreed
>>>**That We**
>>>>Would take a different course.

We entered Earth
>From Realms Above,
>>Without the frame of Time

To function here
>As "**Earthlings**"
>>With a "**Nature**" that's **"Sublime"**.

We knew some things
>Are "Positive"
>>And some are "Negative";

>>>And both are necessary
>>>>So that We could **CHOOSE**
>>>>>**To LIVE!!!**

We needed Both to find
>   Just Who,
>> And Where We **really Are**;

> And to DECIDE that We
>> Could **BE**
>>> The **Light** that came from far!

We're **All** a Part
> Of **That Great Light**
>> That shines where e'er We please.

> For We can make the CHOICE
>> To share
>>> Our **Glorious Frequencies**!!!

YES!!! We *Are*

Within the Being

Of *Our One True Heart!*

We *Are* The One We Were,

And knew,

Right from the start.

We *Are* The Ones Who *Talk,*

And *Laugh,*

And *Love,*

And *Write,*

And *Sing!!!*

We *Are* a part

Of *All That Is,....*

A truly Cosmic Thing!!!!!

Vanessa Conaway Pace
Seattle, Washington, September 30, 2005

Where Am I?

This Is Your Invitation To Create!

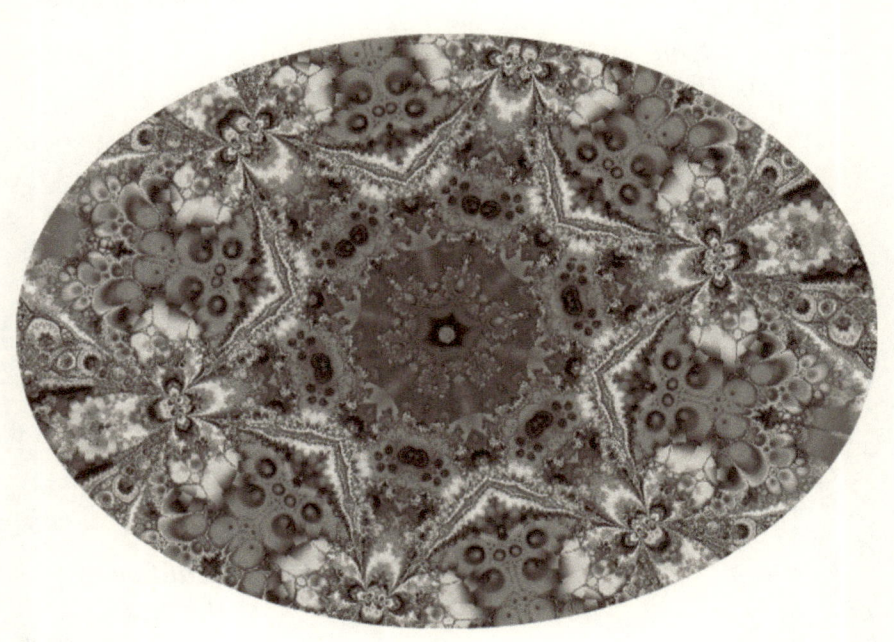

Dear Seeker of Those "Deeper Things",

Since We
    Are All ONE, ...,
        And yet, ...
            A Glorious En-ti-ty,
                Then maybe you
                    Would share a bit
                        Of Your unique
                            I-den-ti-ty

With others
    Who would love
        To find another
            Like themselves,
                For They have also
                    Made some things
                        And stored them
                            On their shelves,

For such a time
    As They would meet
        A kindred soul like You,
            Who'd understand
                The isolation
                    They've
                        Been going through.

They'll let you in
    To their world
        If you'll let them in
            To yours,
                And **that**
                    Would build
                        The highway
                          That would be
                            The end
                              Of wars!!!

Now Its YOUR Turn To Be "Creator"!
Put YOUR Thoughts Here, and Read Them Later!

So, take out your pen,
    And planning device
        And write out
            The Plans
                That will really
                    Be nice!

Now Its YOUR Turn To Be "Creator"!
Put YOUR Thoughts Here, and Read Them Later!

Now Its YOUR Turn To Be "Creator"!
Put YOUR Thoughts Here, and Read Them Later!

*Now Its YOUR Turn To Be "Creator"!
Put YOUR Thoughts Here, and Read Them Later!*

That's A Lot of Rot!

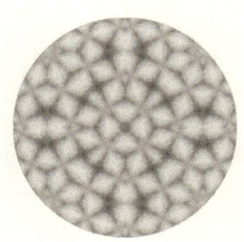

www.pacepublishing.com

"*That's* A Lot of Rot!"
Inspirational Background

    It's tempting to fall into the prescribed mindset that says that there is not enough supply for all of the physical needs of the billions of souls that are here on Planet Earth at this time. And, its tempting to let ourselves off of the hook of the responsible way of life, and drone on with the naysayers that mindlessly pontificate that no matter how hard you work there will never be enough to go around. That kind of negative thinking can quickly degenerate into the ultimate self rejection that says, "Nobody loves me; everybody hates me; I'm going out and eat worms".

    The fear mongers of want and need drone on in their weary babble of the threatened starvation, drought, homelessness, and want for the necessities of life, and hope that we'll help them sing it, because whatever the combined consciousness thinks upon it will create. Its a scenario that was brilliantly depicted by the author Mark Twain in his stories of Tom Sawyer, the well-heeled conformist to society and its restraints, who craftily tries to con the outcast from society, Huck Finn, (the individualistic free soul who cherishes his own freedom, and does what he needs to do to survive), to willingly paint Tom's fence. Like Huck, We're not falling for the lies of shortages, lack, and slavery any more!

The abundance of nature sings a different song!

The great author, publisher, and world-traveled evangelist, Dr. T. L. Osborne awakened my abundance thinking when I read his wonderful book entitled "There is Plenty For Everyone", in which he uses the example of the abundant return that the farmer gets from planting just one kernel of corn. The resulting stock of corn will return hundreds of kernels on the new ears it yields.

He then looks at the multiplicity of beautiful flowers that pop out on the many branches that grow from one flower seed.

We can all observe the copious abundance of uninterrupted Nature. One acorn produces a mighty oak tree, that, in turn, covers the ground around it with a new crop of acorns, that will, in turn, multiply exponentially. The succeeding crops never end,..., **unless someone or something interrupts the natural order of things.**

Trees prolifically reforest Earth's fields and mountains, thus supplying Earth's inhabitants with food, fruits, water, clean air, electromagnetic energy, shade, and shelter, ..., **unless someone or something interrupts the natural cycles.**

We live on a water planet where oceans, clouds, rivers, underground streams, and aquifers supply an abundance of sweet, oxygenated, vibrantly clustered potable water for all to freely drink, ..., **unless someone or something tampers with the free flow of the natural supply.**

As a continuation of his wonderful groundbreaking work on the ability of water to form crystals whose designs out-picture the mood and intention of its observer, famed Japanese researcher Dr. Masaru Emoto (July 22, 1943 – October 17, 2014) tells the story of a river that dried up because of the evil thoughts of one woman! You see, dams are not always *physical!. You can find the story in his book entitled "The Secret Life of Water". ("The Secret Life of Water", by Masaru Emoto, published by ATRIA Book's, New York, and Beyond Worlds Publishing, Inc., Hillsboro, Oregon; translated into English in 2005, pages 117-120.)*

Dr. Emoto was on his first lecture trip to Australia when he was introduced to an aborigine elder to whom he showed the pictures of his photographs of water crystals. The photographs show that the changes in the design and perfection of the frozen water crystals reflected the intention of the person or the music affecting the water. The elder then told Dr. Emoto an ancient tale that had been passed down for generations. In their society it seems that an evil shaman lived at the top of a mountain ridge in New South Wales. A river originated there and flowed down the mountainside, supplying sweet water to all the happy people who lived along the banks of the river. The miserable shaman resented the happiness of the downriver dwellers, and so she copied her thoughts into the water, and filled the river with spite, and the desire that only she would be happy. With her thoughts she blocked the natural flow of the water.

Soon the river dwellers became sick, started bickering, and began fighting among themselves because of the evil thoughts copied into the water by the shaman.

After years of pain and sorrow for the people, one day a young shaman was walking his dog, and the dog began chasing after a kangaroo. When the dog returned it was dripping wet with clean pure water. Curious as to where the water came from, the young shaman followed his dog back up the mountain, and found himself at the door of the evil shaman. From there he could see where the pure water of the river had been blocked.

And so, the story goes, that he turned the evil shaman into water, which began to flow down the mountain. The evil shaman clawed at the edges of the river in an attempt to save herself from being washed into the sea. When finally she grabbed hold of a big rock the young shaman told her that he would save her life if she would change her ways, and work for the good of the people. Miraculously she agreed, and, as they say at the end of all redemptive stories, the people lived happily ever after, with a full supply of sweet, clean water.

The message of this story awakens our memory to the fact that our thoughts affect our physical environment. I was intrigued by a remark a guest made on the late-night talk show "Coast to Coast" wherein he said that energy can be turned into meaninglessness by the symbols we have assigned to it. Wow! The next time you think your life is meaningless, or you are feeling less than empowered, just remember that! We can either use our considerable innate creative powers to build a better world, or, we can succumb to the machinations of others who have learned how to use these energy powers for their nefarious purposes of conquest and control. We must be aware that the blockages in our lives, the situations in our world, and the environmental conditions of the Nature that surrounds us are not always brought into being by things that we can see with the naked eye.

Energy flows freely through the air and can be harnessed for the use of all mankind. It was Nikolai Tesla's dream to freely supply it to the world. He knew, taught, and demonstrated that astronomical amounts of free energy could be harnessed from the atmosphere. I remember Art Bell, talk show host extraordinaire, telling the story of being dangerously knocked about by the free-flowing electricity that had been gathered by his considerable antenna array, and not properly routed harmlessly into the ground. That was some real power!

*Other energy sources come to us from the sun, and even from the universes beyond, and, locally, from the thought forms and intentions of the collective consciousness of man. These could freely meet the energy needs of Earth's population, ..., **unless someone or something captures, redirects, or otherwise interrupts its natural flow***

Abundance, like all of Creation, is not static. The supply is always new, and always available, ..., as long as the laws of its creation are obeyed.

But, sometimes man, the duly deputized personification of The Creator here in the Earth; ...; Man, whose original hard drive seems to have been layered over by some very clever, but misguided, *programmers, sometimes loses his spiritual bearings, and begins to use his innate creative powers in selfish ways, forgetting that his creative powers will work for **de**-struction as well as for **con**-struction. Energy, like money (another form of energy), is neither good nor bad, but simply serves the intentions of its master.*

I like business visionary Stuart Friedman's (president of Progressive Management Associates) definition of abundance: "... the belief there's plenty as long as I take action with purpose and intention and always make progress toward my Specific, Measurable, Action-oriented, Reasonable, and Time-sensitive (SMART) goals", a belief which is opposed by a penchant for scarcity, "..., which means if I get there first I win and you lose...".

Hmmmmmm! You mean that all along abundance was the plan for Earth's inhabitants?

Hmmmmmm! You mean that everything we ever needed or wanted has already been supplied, with a little help from our conformity with the universal laws, but has somehow been redirected by miscreants who understood more about the laws of energy than we have taken the time to study, understand, and wield?

And, if that is the truth, then whose fault is that - the perpetrators, or the ones who failed to do their due diligence about the principles by which all of Creation operates, and then put them into action?

Hmmmmmm! My indignant soul is about to explode. You bet I hear a poem coming on!

www.pacepublishing.com

Poem
"That's A Lot of Rot!"

Where in the world
    Did We ever get the thought
        That We couldn't have
            All that We need?

Now **That's**
    A Lot
        Of Rot!!!

And why would We,
    Who own it all
        Begin to think
            That We're so small

That We would have
    To give it all
        To ones who claim
            There was A "Fall"????

What has made <u>Us</u>
    More inferior
        To them
            Who thought
                Themselves superior
                    To God, ...,
                        Who's Our
                            "Interior"?

Whatever made them think
    That **<u>they</u>**
        Could rule
            While others
                Must obey
                The laws
                    They've made
                        By their own hand
                        So they could rule
                          All ...
                            In the land????

Now, maybe We
    Should stop a bit,
        And seek to learn
            The **Truth** of it.

If all are "**equal**",
    As was said,
        Then **why go down**
            The path they've led??????????????

Where some will work
    And most will toil
        So they can have
            Their "spoil" ...
                Of "**oil**";

And live
    In laps of luxury, ...
        While others
            Pay them usury!!!

There's something wrong!!!
"*Hey!* " "*Wait!*", I said.
"*There's more to Life
Than Daily Bread.*

"*There's dreams,
And Hopes,
And Plans to keep
That **We** must mourn
When ...
We're in so deep!

When others
Of a different "**ilk**"
Have found
Some slaves
They'd like to milk!"*

But, now,
    Before you take up arms
        Or even **think**
            To impose harms
                On those who learned
                    A thing or two
                        And learned
                            To Lord it over You.

Let's be a little
    Smarter than
        That lowest
            Enemy of man
                That makes him act
                    Without a thought
                        Of the destruction
                            That he's bought.

And, let's consider
>   Who We are, ...,

>   **A god,**
>   > That's traveled here
>   > > From far,
>   > > > To learn the craft
>   > > > > Of being **One**
>   > > > > > Of Those Who came out
>   > > > > > > From before **The Sun**.

The Ones of **Light**,

> And **Sound,**

> > And **Love,**

> > > Who have
> > > > Descended
> > > > > From above,

To make this Earth
A better place,
And fit to take
Our place
In Space

With others
Who can live
In **Love**
And **Harmony**
With those above.

Where soon
We'll see
That …
We can't find
Those who
Were of
A **Lower** mind.

They just won't fit
    In what
        Love planned.

    Let Life Begin
        In that NEW LAND!!!!!

Vanessa Conaway Pace
Seattle, Washington, September 16, 2005

That's A Lot Of Rot!!!
Song

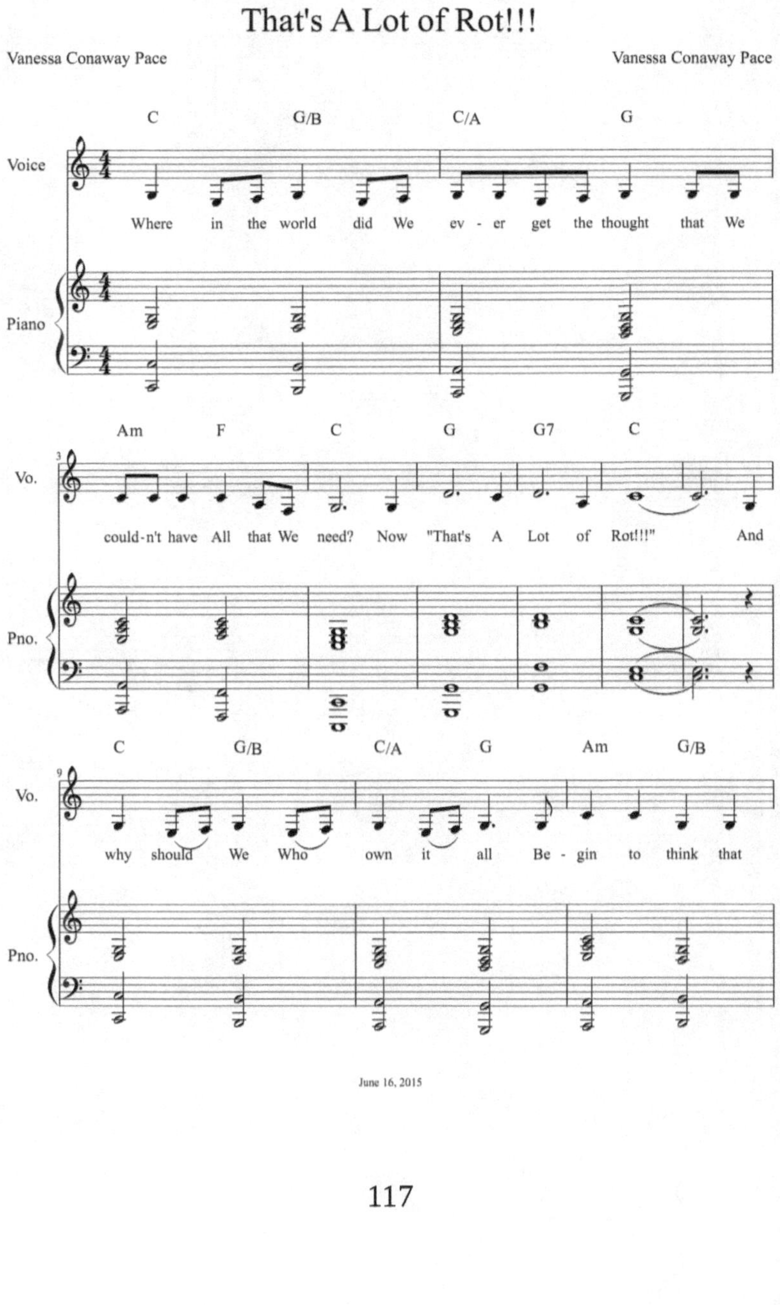

That's A Lot of Rot!!!

Vanessa Conaway Pace Vanessa Conaway Pace

Lyrics:
Where in the world did We ev-er get the thought that We could-n't have All that We need? Now "That's A Lot of Rot!!!" And why should We Who own it all Be-gin to think that

June 16, 2015

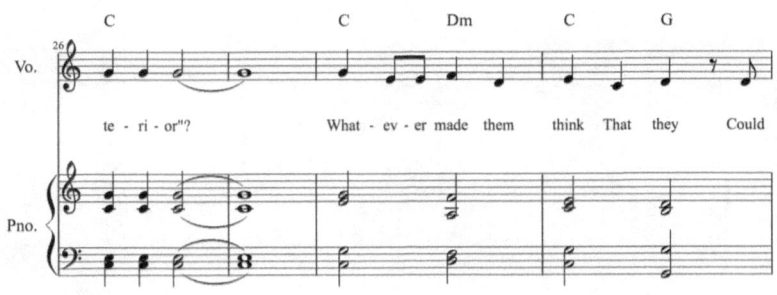
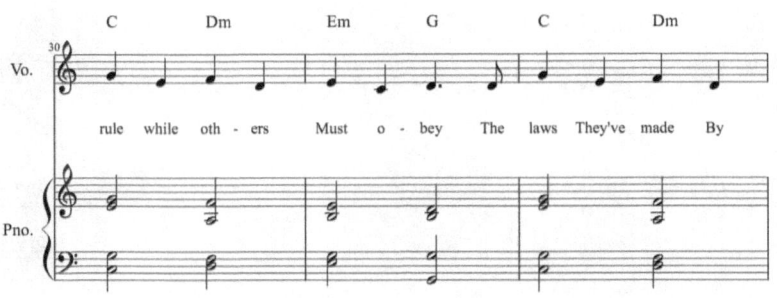

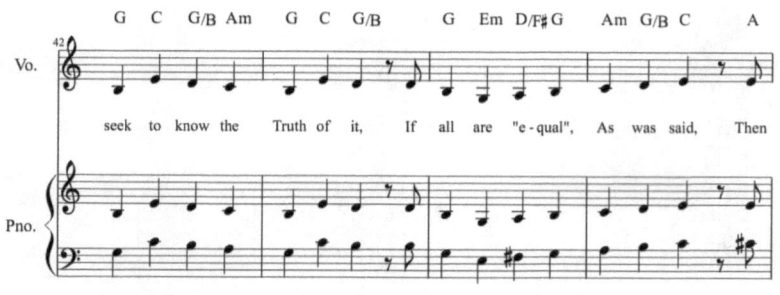

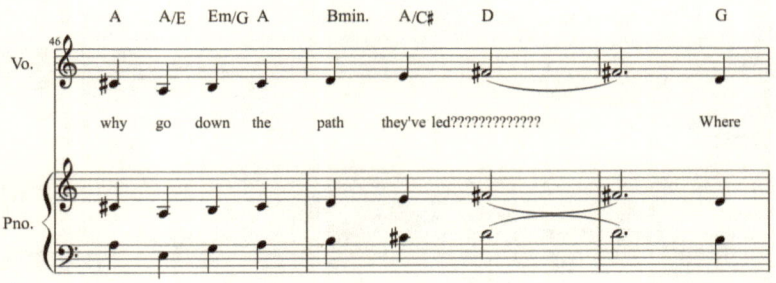

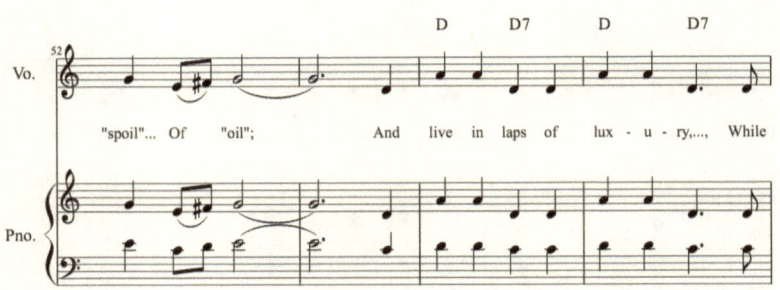

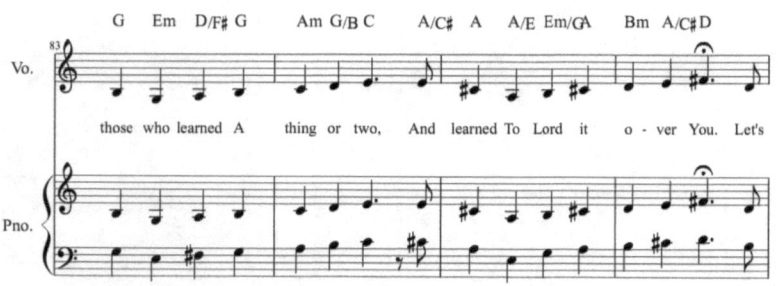
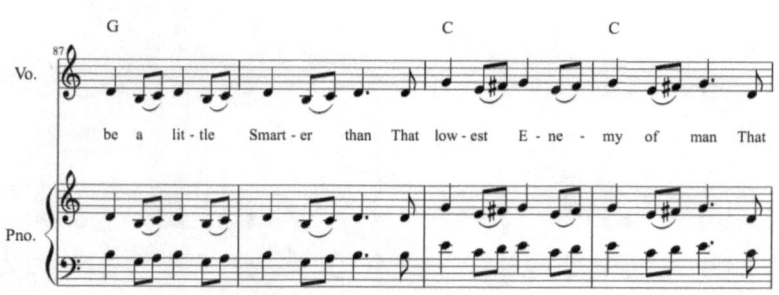

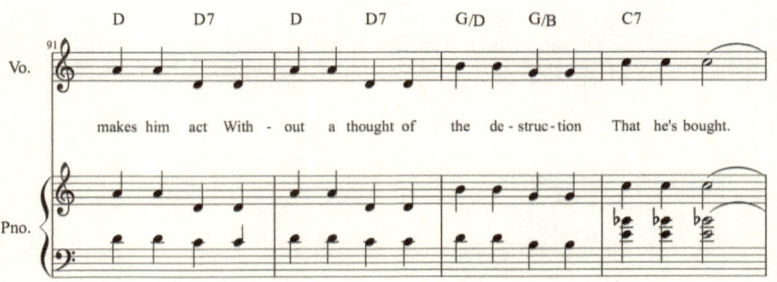

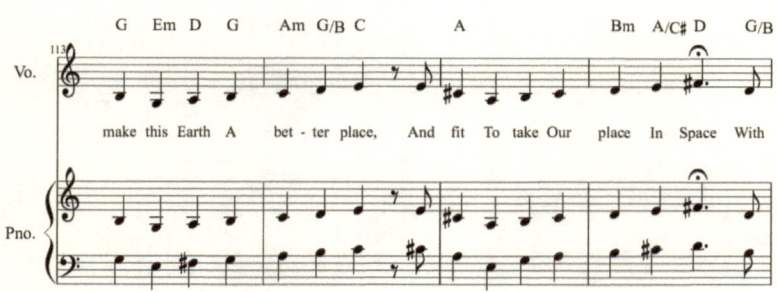

"*That's* A Lot of Rot!"

> *This Is Your*
> *Invitation*
> *To Create!*

Dear Seeker of Those "Deeper Things",

The Dreams,
    And Hopes,
        And Plans
            We mourn
                Were deep
                    Inside
                        When We
                            Were born.

They're planted there
    By **Who** We **are**,
        And what We've always been
           So far,
              And what We've chosen
                To become,
                    (If We could shed
                        The things
                          That numb)

      The feelings
          That We're really **FREE**,
        And, its okay
             Just to **BE "ME"**!!

So, Here's your chance
    To write it down
        Before you start
            To judge, ..., Or frown,
        You just might find
           That it's great fun
        To **see**
            The great thing
                That You've done!

Now Its YOUR Turn To Be "Creator"!
Put YOUR Thoughts Here, and Read Them Later!

Now, grab the pen
    And Book
        You've started,
            And write some ideas
                We've imparted,
                    And **DO** the project, ...,
                        Get it started!!!

Now Its YOUR Turn To Be "Creator"!
Put YOUR Thoughts Here, and Read Them Later!

Now Its YOUR Turn To Be "Creator"!
Put YOUR Thoughts Here, and Read Them Later!

Now Its YOUR Turn To Be "Creator"!
Put YOUR Thoughts Here, and Read Them Later!

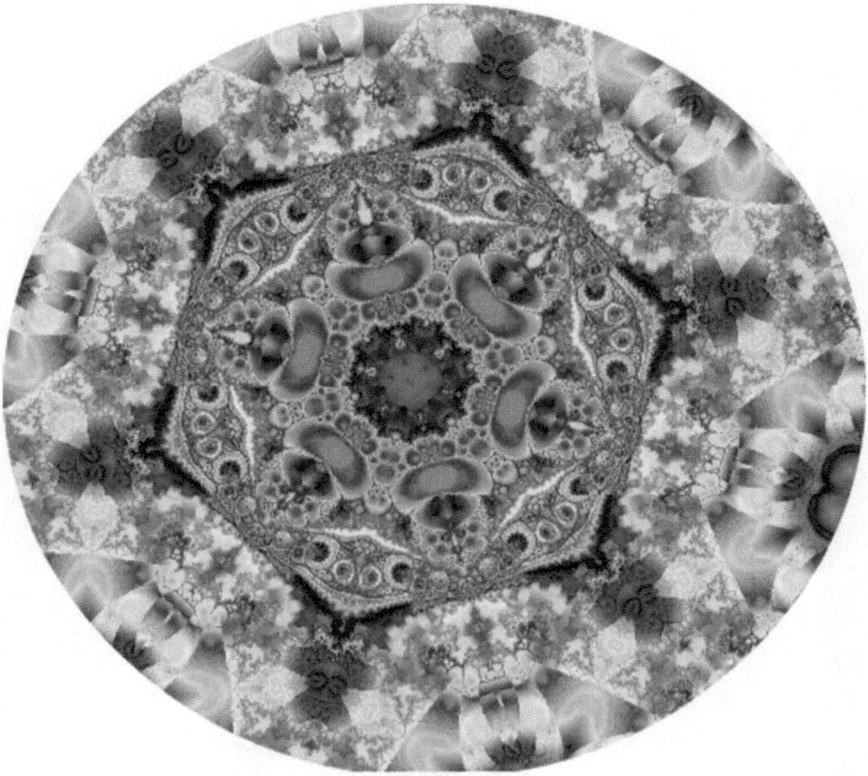

Sound the Trumpet

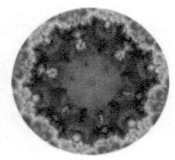

www.pacepublishing.com

"Sound The Trumpet!"
Inspirational Background

> *"He who bloweth not his own horn,*
> *his horn bloweth not."*
> *Abraham Lincoln*

Daddy had escaped the coal mines of West Virginia, and our little family moved to a four acre farm in the country. Both Daddy and Mother were college educated, and both were headed for professional careers, but, both also came from families who had demonstrated the pioneering spirit. One side of the family had braved the rigors of crossing the country in a covered wagon, and the other side of the family had resolutely embarked upon an ocean crossing, both in search of a better and more prosperous, and unhindered life in a new world.

Our move to the open countryside was no less an adventure because my parents left the security of a paycheck from "the company", and faced the unknowns of the life of a farmer. For them, as well as for a myriad of others who value their individual sovereignty, it was independence at any cost. It worked!!! We joined the ranks of the great unsung who have built a better world for themselves and for those who followed. It was not without hardship, fatigue, loneliness, and a real demand upon all the ingenuity we could muster, but, for us, IT WORKED!!!

We sold vegetables, berries, eggs, and chickens along the road to make a living, and to some that put us in a lower level of society. To others, it meant that they could eat good, because everything we sold was first class, organic (before it was fashionable), fresh off the vine, and sold with a smile!

Many people drove from considerable distances to buy our luscious berries, vegetables, chickens, and eggs. I particularly remember this one customer who drove the the 13 miles out from town every Sunday in his fine Cadillac just to buy our direct-from-the-farm produce. He was, shall I say, generously proportioned, ..., my young eyes judging him to more than fill up his side of that luxury car, ..., and, he was always dressed in what we considered superfluous finery for a shopping trip to the country.

Interestingly, his pomposity did not stop with his wrappings. .... While looking down his considerable nose at the lowly farmers who were serving him, he would loudly pontificate on his own greatness. We endured his tirades, collected the much needed money for our precious produce, and then, after he left, laughed at this caricature of worldly pride as we skipped through Mother's lovely flowers, and down the path back to the house, ..., precious and hard-earned money in hand!

Mother and Daddy used those occasions to warn me to stay away from such ones who were filled with themselves, while looking down at those of us who were working for a living. I can still hear Mother's voice quoting Abrahan Lincoln's adage, "He who bloweth not his own horn, his horn bloweth not." I got the message that he who blows himself up with pride gets a little needle in the end!

It was mother's way of teaching me to avoid the unpleasantries of pomposity. Daddy had a more down to earth way of saying it, ..., "If you'd stick a pin in him he'd deflate like a balloon!" They gave me to understand that if you **were** great you wouldn't have to to tell anyone about it, ... They'd figure it out for themselves!

But, maybe Old Abe's witticism actually had a meaning quite different from the one we ascribed to it. Maybe he understood the words of his mouth on a different level. Is it possible that our patriotic countryman understood things at a deeper level of life than we country bumpkins understood it? Maybe he had looked at things through a more advanced level of appreciation for "tooting your own horn". The knowledge of the power and usage of sound as a creative force has been around for a long time ... at least for some!

Trumpets are among the oldest musical instruments, dating back to at least 1500 BC. They are a member of the brass family, and play the highest notes. Bronze and silver trumpets were found in King Tut's tomb in Egypt, and metal trumpets in China date back to the same time. Trumpets were important to societies who had no electronic means of communications. In those days they were not used for "music" in the modern *sense, but, rather, they were used for military or religious purposes,. Their playing was so valuable to society that it was a guarded craft in medieval times, with its instruction being passed on only within the members of highly selective guilds. It is interesting that the trumpet players were often among the most heavily guarded members of the troop, because they were relied upon to relay instructions to other sections of the Army. It was necessary to be able to communicate specific instructions over large distances, and the voice of the trumpet would carry across the mountains and the valleys.*

There were many types of trumpets, each being designed to fulfill its specific purpose. The herald trumpet is the most showy member of the trumpet family . It has a long shaft from which banners or flags are usually hung, and it is mostly used for ceremonial events such as parades and fanfares.

I remember wonderful musical evenings during my summers in Washington D.C. Summers there are hot and muggy, and any break from their oppression is openly welcomed. Those evenings were particularly exciting because from the giant barge that had been stationed on the Potomac River in front of the Lincoln Memorial beautiful and stirring music would be played by the National Symphony Orchestra, or the US Army or Navy Bands and Choruses. The emancipated office workers who had braved the rigors of snail-paced traffic to cool off to the strains of great music were always rewarded.

I had two particular musical favorites, and always made sure that I was there when they were on the program. One of them was by the famous Russian composer, Modest Mussorgsky, entitled "The Great Gate of Kiev", which always electrified all with its use of real military cannons to heighten the celebratory ending of the piece. That wasn't something a girl from the hills of West Virginia experienced every day! And then there was the drama of the "Fanfare for the Common Man", which Aaron Copeland wrote for herald trumpets with orchestra. The sight and sound of an array of herald trumpeters that stretched all the way across the front of that great barge called every goose bump in the crowd to full muster! There's nothing like the command of a herald trumpet. Your very bones hear it, And its clarion call requires your response. Such is the power of the trumpet.

The sound of the trumpet is like no other. Its penetrating sound waves demand a hearing, and the message the trumpet brings penetrates deeply into the furthest recesses of our Being. We are immediately on alert, and we instinctively know that something important is afoot. That quality has made the trumpet, and it's trumpeter, a valued part of armies the world over. Without the trumpet the troops didn't march. Without the trumpet messages could not be delivered over long distances. Yes, those penetrating notes from the highest sounding member of the brass family of instruments rallied the troops, and the familiar melodies detailed the tasks they were to perform. For example, when the trumpeter plays "Reveille" the troops know its time to get up.

The trumpeter initiates the musical vibrations that are then amplified by the trumpet, and they call a response from the people that hear that trumpet sound. The same process can also be initiated by **OUR OWN VOICE!** <u>Our</u> <u>Voice</u> <u>is</u> <u>Our</u> <u>Hu-man</u> <u>Trumpet!!</u> What works for the trumpeter works for US!!!

As was quoted at the beginning of this chapter, "He who bloweth not his own horn, his horn bloweth not." Abraham Lincoln was right after all!!!

Therefore, it seems quite logical to me that, if "The trumpet **shall** sound, ..., it will come out of **YOU**!", as it says in the following poem, then it must come out of **US**, the **living trumpets**!!! That means that each person has a unique responsibility, that only **THEY** can initiate, to sound their own trumpet, and to proclaim their **own** message.

Oh, my!! It's up to "Me" again. It seems that it's always up to "Me"! It seems that this universal system always tags "Me" as the responsible one! "I AM Creator", as said in the earlier poem in this book. I set the "wheels" of my world into motion by the vibrations I send out by MY Thoughts, My Emotions, and My Voice, and the quality of them will be very obvious to all by the tune my trumpet plays!

Oh, boy! I feel the trumpet's blast of a poem coming on!!!

www.pacepublishing.com

Poem
Sound The Trumpet!

Sound The Trumpet,
>   As You have been told;
>>   **Sound** a *clarion* call,
>>>   Stand right up, and be bold!

Yes! Lift up **Your Voice**
>   And declare Your commands.
>>   **Let them travel the paths**
>>>   **Of the energy bands.**

Sound the alarm
>   **On a mighty broad band**
>>   That will join with the Choir
>>>   All across the land.

Let the *airwaves* ring
>   With the **sound** of **Your Voice**
>>   That will sweep the air clean
>>>   As You shout out Your choice!

Let the innocent message
 Of **Love**,
  And of **Grace**,
   Travel far
    On the wings
     Of **Your song**
      Throughout space.

Then the airwaves
 Will take it,
  And send it,
   As planned,
    'Til it reaches the ears
     And the heart
      Of each man.

And together
 We'll draw Them,
  And cause **Them** to **sing**
   Of the Love,
    And the Joy,
     And the Peace
      That **We** bring.

And They, too,
> Will become
>> What We've
>>> Secretly planned; ...
>>>> ...**Another strong Voice,**
>>>>> **On another broad band!**

Each in the bandwidth
> To which They're assigned;
>> All sounding together
>>> As **One Music Mind;**

The **Song of Creation,**
> And of **Those of Great Might**
>> All taking Their part
>>> **In the Spectrum**
>>>> **Of Light!**

For We're building a **Choir**
    That will meld
        As **one sound!**

        Let the Heavens,
          The Earth,
             All Creation resound!

Let Their sound waves
    All mingle,
        Their tones multiply;
        For **UNITED**,
           Not single,
               They'll traverse
                The sky!

Be faithful to share
    What You've known
        From before,
        That will open
           The **Secrets of Voice**
              Even more!

There is much more to know
    Of the pow'r
        Of the **Voice,**
            And in seeking
                This knowledge
                    You've made
                        The right choice!

Step out even further!
    Launch out from the shore,
        And We'll share
            From the
                Treasures of Song
                Even more!

For You've been given weapons,
    That equipped You
        With might,
            And granted You power
                To turn darkness
                    To **Light!**

So, **Sing Out the Glory**

    That is placed

        Within!

It is CREATIVE POWER!!!

    Let CREATION begin!!!!!

Command things

    That are not

        To come into place;

            And to things

                That should NOT be

            Sing words

                  That ERASE!

For The Trumpet **Shall** Sound...

    It will come <u>**out of You!**</u>

        Since **You** bear

            Light's Great Glory

                To thine own Self

                Be true!

Just follow The Plan
    That We have arranged;
        And stay right on course,

    For **NOTHING'S**
        BEEN CHANGED!!!

                Vanessa Conaway Pace
           Seattle, Washington, September 29, 2005

www.pacepublishing.com

Sound The Trumpet

This Is Your Invitation To Create!

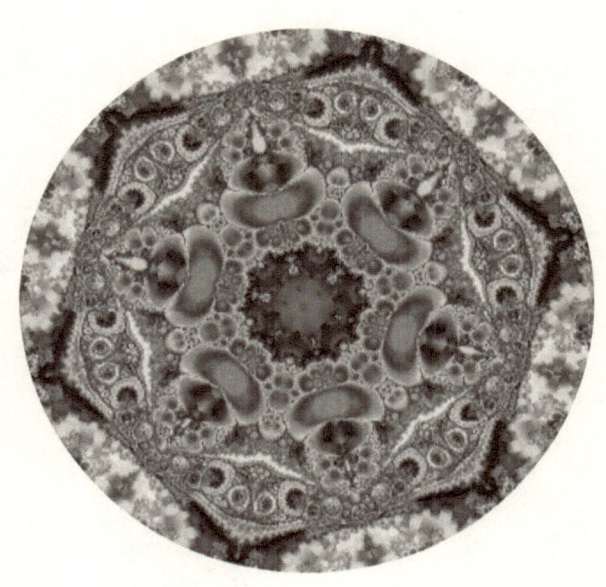

Dear Seeker of Those "Deeper Things",

"To thine own self be true",
    Is the message, for sure,
        So, until you will **DO that**
            We'll have to endure
                The emptiness left
                    In the space
                        You can fill
            With the thoughts
                And the plans,
                    And the works
                        Of your **Will.**

There's a Treasure
    That's there
        On the inside of **You;**
            And the hunt for it
                Might take
                    A moment, ..., or two!

But You'll see
    It's well worth it
        When you stand back
        And look
            At the song You created, ...,
                The picture, ...,
                Or book

That you made
    By your own hand, ...,
        Or sang with your Voice, ...,
        Or You wrote, ...,
            Or You painted, ..., ...,
                Make Creation
                    Your choice!

Now Its YOUR Turn To Be "Creator"!
Put YOUR Thoughts Here, and Read Them Later!

Remember The Book
    That You started
        In the beginning?

  Now, get it out
      And add
         A new inning

      In the game of Life
         Where We create
        It all,

        And, remember,
           There is nothing
              Too big
                  Or too small!

Now Its YOUR Turn To Be "Creator"!
Put YOUR Thoughts Here, and Read Them Later!

Now Its YOUR Turn To Be "Creator"!
Put YOUR Thoughts Here, and Read Them Later!

Now Its YOUR Turn To Be "Creator"!
Put YOUR Thoughts Here, and Read Them Later!

Am I ??? ... ...

www.pacepublishing.com

"Am I ??? ... ..."
Inspirational Background

Maybe there is more to us than the eye can see. Maybe we really are more complex Beings than we have ever considered that we could possibly be.

Days are busy, and schedules are full, so often times we are required to multi-task in order to get everything done before our time and energies run out for the day. Part of us is talking on the phone, while another part of us is preparing dinner, while another part of us is helping the children with their homework, while behind the scenes another part of us may be listening to music, memorizing a talk that we must give, or planning what we will wear to work the next day.

We get it all done, so obviously we are created as multifaceted Beings, and we can function on many different levels. Somehow, in my conservative upbringing, I always thought I would be able to see and experience all those different parts of "Me" and appreciate the genius of it all!

Yes, we are people of many voices. And, just being aware of that fact makes us want to tune up each one of them so they will all sing together in a glorious life Symphony. We are a bit like those magnificent eight-part Chorales that Johann Sebastian Bach (and others) so masterfully put together. Each of the eight parts, which are called "Voices", has its own particular genius, and without it justice has not been done to the composition, and the performance is not complete. (His "Christmas Oratorio" is one marvelous example.) And, neither are We complete unless our many Voices remain intimately connected to, and actively singing together in the Great Composition and Performance that is "My Life's Song".

I can easily relate to that concept of the whole person. There are so many parts of me, many gifts and talents within me, and each has each clamored for development over the years. And I have many interests that have taken me on marvelous adventures of learning and experience. But what shall I actually BE?

My practical mind, fueled by the programming of my society's accepted mores, was telling me that I must irreversibly choose a path, a career, and most importantly, choose a steady job. Even if I didn't enjoy it, it would be a steady income so I could pay the bills.

I was grieving the loss of all those other skills and interests that I had developed, should I succumb to the dictum to choose just ONE. Was it all in vain? Would I forever be stuck in some dead end career, mindlessly building the bricks of someone else's dream (read "demands"), and consequently relegated to that end-of-life dead end that they've created called "retirement". The glories of Nature do not picture such an option. Nor does Nature support anything that is not producing new life. Every living thing has its purposeful function in life, and continuously contributes to the ongoing growth of the planet

No! I wanted to follow a more upward-bound path, going from glory to glory as I ascended back up into the awesome Creative Being of my Origin, ..., ever recovering the brilliance of the Source from whence I came. I envisioned passages from the lesser states of my understandings and abilities to greater levels of mastery, self-discipline, and achievement. How could I abandon all those fascinating parts of "Me", and just follow ONE?

My grief process (with maybe a little stubborn resistance thrown in) was interrupted by a new idea that I gleaned from yet another important book in my life. The author's fresh look on life advised that we must choose ONE interest in life,..., one pursuit that truly excites us, and for which our passion would lead us into the depths of discovery, ..., and then, all around and out of that impassioned pursuit all other interests, gifts, and talents would be drawn upon to bring that Life Work into completion.

Ahhhh! I could use it all! The combined elements of "Me" would make a greater whole!

I made the choice. For me it would be the things that excite me most - Singing! ..., Voice! ..., Poetry! ..., All of those creative aspects of Music!!!

No sooner had I heaved a sigh of relief, knowing that none of it had been wasted, I was introduced to the concept of parallel universes! Oh, dear! Could all of those divergent paths that I had explored really have led to other "Me's" in other dimensions? Oh! That IS a stretch!!!

I found a definition of parallel universes that I could work with: "A parallel universe is a hypothetical self-contained separate reality co-existing with one's own." Hmmm. It seems that parallel universes take place in the same space and time as our own universe, but we have no way to access them. Hmmm. They say that every moment of our life, every decision we make, causes a split of our "now" cells into an infinite number of future selves, all of which are unaware of each other.

Far out! *You mean that when my friend in far away London called me to say that she was sure that she had seen me in London that day, that maybe she could be right? You mean that when I started thinking about going to see her, and then changed my mind, I actually created that thought form, and in another universe that* scenario actually played out, and is still playing itself out? Whoa! I wonder how many universes my active mind has created!

I always look for proofs and confirmations of such intrusions upon my conservatively well-educated mind. It is January 10, 2015, in Seattle as I ponder these things. Because of the differing Time Zones, it is January 11, 2015, in far-away London, and I see via the Internet that today's "Daily Mail" carries an article with this headline: "'Parallel universes DO exist': Multiple versions of us are living in alternate worlds that interact with each other, theory claims".

Wow!!! Confirmation from far-away London, in the daily newspaper, that these thoughts may be worth considering. Hmmmmm!

Oh dear! I do hear a poem coming on!

Poem
Am I ??? ...? ...?

Am I the One
> Who dreams at night
>> And travels far and wide?

Or Am I just
> The Earthbound One
>> That's locked inside this hide?

Am I a soul
> From ancient times
>> Who's seen a thing or two?

Or am I just
> A lump of clay
>> That hasn't got a Clue?!!

Am I a form
> That's happening now
>> With only this one chance?

Or am I here
> To **choose** my fate? ...

... A Joyous happenstance!!!!

Am I across the ocean
    When I seem
        To understand
            The heart of One
                I've known before
                    In some far distant land?

Or, am I rooted
    To this spot
        That's tangible,
            And firm?

The thought
    That we might
        "<u>Float around</u>"
            Would surely
                Make us squirm!!!

Am I a finite Being
>   With beginning,
>   >   And sure end?

Or,
>   Am I part
>   >   Of ALL THAT IS?

Its hard to comprehend!!!!

Vanessa Conaway Pace
Seattle, Washington, July, 2005

www.pacepublishing.com

Am I ??? ...? ...?

> ***This Is Your Invitation To Create!***

Dear Seeker of Those "Deeper Things",

"Am I" DOING
    The things
        That I came here
            To DO,
                Or, "Am I"
                    Lazing around
                        Like a comfy
                            Old shoe?

"Am I" daring
    To risk
        All I AM
            Just to **BE**
                This wondrous expression
                    Of **"ME"**
                        That I see?

That is loaded
    With "**Life**"
        That came here
            And "Became"; ...,
                ..., If it did,
                    And that's true,
                        Then We must
                            Up our game!

So, take these next pages
    As a space
        To emplace
            The Face
                Of Your place
                    In this Earthbound
                        Airspace!!!

Now Its YOUR Turn To Be "Creator"!
Put YOUR Thoughts Here, and Read Them Later!

Remember The Book
    That We started before?

        Now, pick it up,
            And Your pen,
                And write ideas
                    Galore!

Now Its YOUR Turn To Be "Creator"!
Put YOUR Thoughts Here, and Read Them Later!

Now Its YOUR Turn To Be "Creator"!
Put YOUR Thoughts Here, and Read Them Later!

Now Its YOUR Turn To Be "Creator"!
Put YOUR Thoughts Here, and Read Them Later!

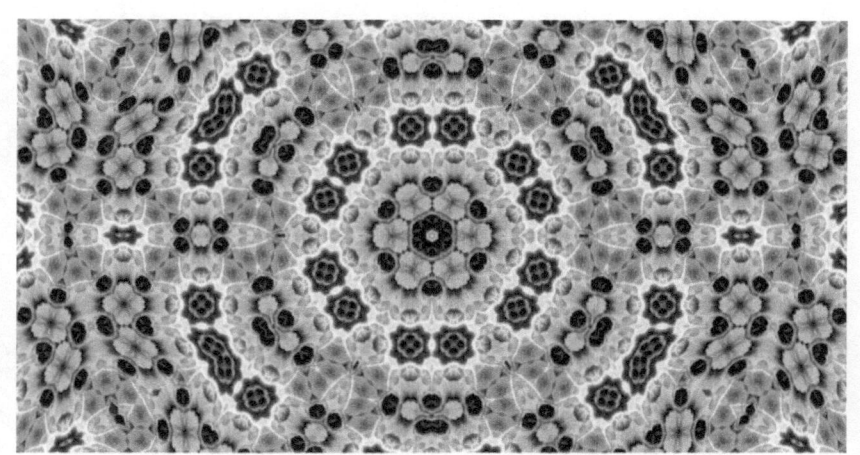

Green Seasons

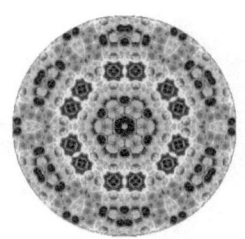

www.pacepublishing.com

"Green Seasons"
Inspirational Background

We're learning
> The lessons
>> That We planned,
>>> But Ohhhhhhh!
>>>> The progress
>>>>> We're making
>>>>>> Seems painfully
>>>>>>> Slow.

We take three steps
> Forward,
>> Then two paces
>> Back,
>>> Because
>>>> We start thinking
>>>>> Of sickness
>>>>>> And lack,

And find Ourselves
　　　Right back
　　　　　In our comfy scene
　　　　　　　Of old ways,
　　　　　　　　　Which really
　　　　　　　　　　　Were NOT
　　　　　　　　　　　　　All that keen.

We slip into thinking
　　　The gossip
　　　　　And Woe
　　　　　　　Of letters
　　　　　　　　　We've written
　　　　　　　　　　　A long time ago,

And stories
　　　We let others
　　　　　Dump in our ear,
　　　　　　　As they spread
　　　　　　　　　Their depressions
　　　　　　　　　　　Year after year....

And We
>   Joined right in,
>> Like a negative Dope,
>>> And soon
>>>> We were both
>>>>> On that slippery slope

That creates
> A "thought form"
>> That leads to despair,
>>> And all of it came
>>>> 'Cause we chemtrailed
>>>>> Our air!

Yes!
> We **<u>did</u>**
>> With our thoughts,
>>> And the words
>>>> That we spoke
>>>>> What We blamed
>>>>>> Others for,
>>>>>>> And THAT
>>>>>>>> Is no joke!

We used
    All the force
        Of our Creative Genius
            In a negative way
                That could only
                    Demean us!

Then the pain
    Brought us back
        To our need
            For a cure
                When the throbbing
                    Got so bad
                        We could not
                            Endure.

Then our
    Lightning fast mind said,
        "Hey, wait,
            It's not working; ... ;
                Everywhere I turn
                    It seems
                        Trouble's lurking!

So then,

    We start searching

        Outside of ourselves,

            Hoping Santa

                Will send us

                    Some help

                        From his Elves.

And ***that***

    Never comes,...,

        Not to our

            Satisfaction;...;

                But ***that's***

                    What has led me

                        To take

                            Spirit action!

Yes! ***That's***

    When I knew

        That there is nothing outside

            Of the flesh

                That I'm wearing

                    That can be

                      My guide.

The "Real Me"
    That's looking
        At you
            Through these eyes
                Is the One
                    Who must shatter
                        My outside
                            Disguise,

And turn
    My gaze inward,
        Where **Real Truth**
            Is stored,
                Along with
                    The lifeline
                        To my Higher Lord.

Who's waiting there,
    Patiently,
        Hoping I'll ask
            If there is
                A "Wiser Me"
                    Under this mask.

So **We**
    Can converse
        About Life,
            Love, and things,
                And I'll
                    Be made wiser
                        By the answers
                            This brings.

I'll learn how
    To make
        Our lives better
            While here
                In the stifling air
                    Of Earth's
                        Atmosphere.

Yes! There are
    "Greener Seasons"
        Awaiting to bloom,
            So, let's all
                Learn how
                    We can give them
                        More room,

To make Earth's air
> Much sweeter,
>> Her waters more pure
>>> Where all men
>>>> Can choose
>>>>> From her blessings
>>>>>> Du jure.

It will all come,
> When **WE**
>> Learn the Law
>>> Of Attraction,
>>>> And start putting
>>>>> Our Creative Powers
>>>>>> Into ACTION!

When **WE**
> Learn to give **Voice**
>> To that which
>>> We want,
>>>> With the courage
>>>>> Of One
>>>>>> Who is quite
>>>>>>> Confidant,

And We truly
    Discover
        That energy flows
            In the way
                Its directed
                    By someone
                        Who KNOWS,...,

*Then **We'll***
    Wield the power
        Of that principle,
            *And **We'll** create*
                A Life
                    That is
                        Extra-dimensional;

No more held
    In the boundaries
        Others have set,
            That would
                Dumb us all down
                    So We'd be
                        In their debt,

But, *free*
> To Become
>> All We've longed for
>>> Before,
>>>> And to know
>>>>> How to consciously
>>>>>> Rise up
>>>>>>> And soar!

...!

Oh, I do hear a poem coming on!

Poem
"Green Seasons"

The seasons may come
    And the seasons may go
        (They're going much faster
            These days, don't you know?)

But the seasons **these** days
    Are becoming more **green**
        With greater things happ'ning
            Than we've ever seen!

The blessings are greater
    The promises **SURE!**
        The pathway grows brighter
            For those that endure.

Where once there was darkness
    We now can see light!
        Where once there was sadness
            Its met with a fight!

Where once there was gloom
　And a touch of despair
　　Our eyes behold **New Life!**
　　　For **The Truth** brings it there!

Where once there was heartache
　And torment, and pain
　　Now there's **accomplishment,**
　　Purpose,
　　　And **gain!!!**

Oh, Yes! It's a **new** day!
　　Now **Hope** has a **Voice!**
　　　With Victories coming!
　　　It's a matter of Choice!

So gird up your life
　　With the Knowledge of **Truth**
　　　And you'll find to your comfort
　　　It isn't a spoof!

For all that was promised
>   We really did mean
>   So We will soon live
>   In that Heavenly scene!

For The **New** Day is coming!
>   It's nigh at the door
>   **Let Your Voices be heard**
>   **With one mighty roar.**

Let's proclaim that **Love's** Power
>   Now rules in the Earth
>   And all that's been planned
>   **Is now coming**
>   **To birth!**

This **new** way is better!
>   **And full of reward!**
>   **And life's more exciting...**
>   **You'll never be bored!**

Vanessa Conaway Pace
Seattle, Washington, October 3, 2005

www.pacepublishing.com

Green Seasons

> ***This Is** Your*
> ***Invitation**
> **To Create!***

Dear Seeker of Those "Deeper Things",

You've struggled
    And studied,
        And started,
            And stopped,
                And felt that your efforts
                    Have all been
                        Sweat-shopped.

But I'm here
    To tell you
        That New Life's
            Beginning, and
                Ones such as You
                    Will begin
                        To be Winning!!

This New Day is coming
    Because We required it,
        And our cries for some help here
            Have really inspired it;

So, now is the time
    To run for the goal,
        And to ignite every coal
            Smoldering deep
                In Your Soul.

Let the fire
    Of your dreams
        Spread their burn
            To these pages
                And then follow the steps
                    Of its logical stages;

And soon
    You will see
        That the Project
           you've started
                Is now moving ahead, ...,
                    ..., Like the Sea
                        Has been parted!

It just took some planning
    And pressing on in
        To make it all happen!
Let Your great work
Begin!!!

Now Its YOUR Turn To Be "Creator"!
Put YOUR Thoughts Here, and Read Them Later!

Remember the Planning Book
    That We've begun?

        Go get it!
            And let it
                Record
                    All the fun!

Now Its YOUR Turn To Be "Creator"!
Put YOUR Thoughts Here, and Read Them Later!

Now Its YOUR Turn To Be "Creator"!
Put YOUR Thoughts Here, and Read Them Later!

Now Its YOUR Turn To Be "Creator"!
Put YOUR Thoughts Here, and Read Them Later!

*Now Its YOUR Turn To Be "Creator"!
Put YOUR Thoughts Here, and Read Them Later!*

Light

www.pacepublishing.com

"Light"
Inspirational Background

    Sometimes the problems of this world that we live in seem a bit out of control and overwhelming, and we resign ourselves to an insidious despair of ever being able to do anything about it. We feel unknown and powerless, so we reason that we may as well learn to live with the status quo, and just make the best of it.

    *Is it all really that hopeless? Is there anything that one person, or one small group of people can do to throw a little **"Light"** into the darkness? Salman Khan thought so.*

    Wikipedia tells us that he was born and raised in New Orleans, Louisiana, to a father from Bangladesh, and a mother from Calcutta, India.. "After earning three degrees from the Massachusetts Institute of Technology (a BS in mathematics, a M.Sc. in electrical engineering and computer science, and an MEng in electrical engineering and computer science) he pursued an MBA from Harvard Business School. In late 2004, Khan began tutoring his cousin Nadia in mathematics using Yahoo's

Doodle notepad. When other relatives and friends sought similar help he decided it would be more practical to distribute the tutorials on YouTube. Their popularity there and the testimonials of appreciative students prompted Khan to quit his job in finance..., and focus on the tutorials...." And, as they say, the rest is history. Students from around the world have eagerly sought his on-line teachings. (www.khanacademy.org)

Again Wikipedia tells us, "Khan Academy is a nonprofit educational organization created in 2006 by educator Salman Khan to provide **'a free, world-class education for anyone, anywhere'.... All resources are available for free to anyone around the world.**" Salman Khan opens his website (www.khanacademy.org) with the hopeful message that **"You only have to know one thing: You can learn anything"**.

I remember being in Rwanda a few years after the 1994 genocide, and traveling through the grief stricken nation. In village after village the adult and professional members of the community had been hideously murdered, leaving children to care for and educate other children. Any professional teachers who had survived had been moved up to the higher grades so that at least there could be some education for the older children in the country.

I saw the great need for education, but how to deliver it to isolated and rural areas where they had no reliable access to electricity or modern communications. I envisioned prerecorded teachings which could be sent through the airwaves and pulled down by anyone who had a simple radio. There was no time to prepare a whole new bevy of teachers; nor was it feasible to bring in large numbers of previously trained teachers over those dusty roads. To me, broadcasts of classes over the airwaves was a do-able beginning, ..., a simple solution that would begin to bring much coveted education to children whose lives had already been irreparably devastated. We had to help. We had to start somewhere. And so I cried out in great desperation for ways and means to supply such prerecorded and electronically delivered courses for the people who could not travel to distant schools. Yes, I came back from that trip determined to help. And, we wrote a 318 page Guidebook entitled "For The Love Of Children: A Guidebook For Early Childhood Education", to train and equip anyone to be practical Preschool Teachers in disadvantaged situations (available in both book format and as an audio-book on www.amazon.com , and from www.pacepublishing.com) and we began the arduous task of getting it to the people.

But the universe was way ahead of me! Even before I sent out the call for help, Salman Khan was already sharpening up his skills, so that he could be equal to the task of providing his on-line Academy, and **"a free, world-class education for anyone, anywhere"**! The collective energies of a desperate people, and the others who came, and saw the need, and cared, combined into a mighty rushing stream of energy that created the answers that they, and others around the world, needed. Can one man make a difference? Can YOU make a difference? Salman Khan is lighting a candle, and making the Earth a better place for many, who, but for his efforts, would be stumbling in the dark.

A 1950's hit song croons,
> "It is better to light just one little candle,
> Than to stumble in the dark".

It became a great hit song for the velvet voice of singer Perry Como, and its composer George Mysel and lyricist Joseph Maloy Roach. And it's a song that is worth looking up and reviving because its hauntingly beautiful melody sings out a great Truth. It invites us all to sing the profound message that We could bring this spaceship called Earth that We live on, into the wonderful Enlightenment that we would like to enjoy, simply by all joining together as one great voice singing out that intension. Imagine a world ringing with the song of the heart cry of the longed for peace, love, and Light that all sane, sensitive, and seeking Hu-mans are longing for!

We want peace. We are weary to the bones of war,..., any kind of "war", whether it's within our own self, between husbands and wives, between parents and children, or siblings, or friends, governments and their enslaved people, nation against nation, or StarWars that most of us are still having a hard time acknowledging even exist. (But, why would history mention them so often if they hadn't existed?)

We want Love,..., Love coming in, and Love going out. Since we have come from The Source, Who **IS** Love, then we are made of the same stuff, and, therefore, must **BE** Love also. We must find ways to give **and** receive those same "Love vibes", lest we wither up and die on the vine of Life.

And, by the same token, We **want "Light"**. **"Light"** coming in, and **"Light"** going out. Since We have come from The Source, Who **IS "Light"**, then We are made of the same stuff, and, therefore, must **BE "Light"**. We must find ways to give **and** receive those same "**Light**" vibes, lest we stumble and fall in the darkness that we have allowed.

"Allowed"? **"Allowed"**, you say? How could we mere Earth-dwellers have **"allowed"** darkness to exist in our Edenic end of the Galaxy? Surely it was **put upon us** by some outside malevolent force.

The song that was so well received by the battle weary people who were trying to put the horrors of World War II behind them gives us a clue. It closes with the promising lines,

"And if every one lit just one little candle
What a bright world this would be."

I challenge you to recognize that the **"Light" within you** is a marvelous tool that, if you will but dare to use it, will be a much welcomed power source that will help make the Earth shine with a brighter **"Light"**. Surprise of all surprises, **only We can make the darkness "Light"!!!** <u>**The Dynamo for running the power plants of Earth is actually within Her people!**</u> When we awaken to the sobering fact of that Truth We will enlighten the darkness that we have **"allowed"** because we didn't understand the system and how it works. <u>**We are the only source of "Light" here.**</u> That's <u>**why**</u> we're here! There was a need to enlighten the darkness, and We knew We could do it! As We are remembering who We are, and from whence We came, We are each turning up the flame on our candle, and the whole world will be able to see and recognize its own glories in that bright *"Light"*!

Hmmmm. Think I'll turn this ray of "Light" into the shape of a poem!!

Poem
Light

Light ...
    Shines in the "darkness",
        But the "darkness"
            *Has no **Light**.*

So, the one who thinks
    That he can live
        In "darkness"
            Ain't too bright!!

*'Cause its **Light***
    *That gives Us **Life***
        *Which is **The Source***
            From whence We came;
So, the one
    Who seeks the "darkness"
        Doesn't understand
        The Game!!

We came from **Light,**
    So don't you think
        There's just a little bit
            Of that old **Flame**
                That came *in* Us
                    That kinda
                        Keeps us
                            "Lit"?!!

Now, if even one small candle
    Can make the "darkness" hide,
        How can there be
            A "darkness"
                Near ... **The Ones**
                    With **Light Inside??!**

So, maybe we should
    Stop and think
        About a thing or two
            That we were told
                In that **old school**
                    That tried to hide
                        This Clue!

Its **Light**

    That is The Source of All

        And **IT**

            Was spawned

                By **Sound**.

Now, isn't **that**

    A funny thing?

        What goes around,

            Comes round!!!

For **Sound**

    Revved up,

        Is **Color**, ...,

    Then is **Light**,

        Which gives the **Life**

           That gave the **Sound**

                That makes the **Light**

                That makes

                    The "darkness"

                        Bright!!!

Its All **One Source,** ...

        The All In All, ...,

    The One

        Of Power And Might.

And **We**

    Are **They**

        Who came From **All.**

        <u>**We**.....</u>

        Make the "darkness"

        Light!!!!!!!

Vanessa Conaway Pace
Seattle, Washington, September 16, 2005

Light

> *This Is Your*
> *Invitation*
> *To Create!*

Dear Seeker of Those "Deeper Things",

So, now we know
    There is "**Light**" inside,
        And there is no place where "**Light**"
        Can run and hide!
    Now, may be You **will** think
        To Shine "**Light**" you've plied
            To all that's around You
                In a true sense of pride.
...

You are
    The One
        That came
            Equipped
                With some
                    Exciting skill
            That You
                Can share
                    With others.......
                        Oh!! I surely hope
                          You will!!!

So, while You're in
    The mood for it
        I hope You'll
            Write it down,
                And nurture it
                    With Faithfulness,...,
                  ..., Your seeds
                    Of great
                      Renown!

Now Its YOUR Turn To Be "Creator"!
Put YOUR Thoughts Here, and Read Them Later!

There's something
      Very deep inside
           That You
                No longer
                     Need to hide.

    So, grab that Book
          We've started here,
               And write down
                    All Your thoughts,...,
                        Then Cheer!!!

Now Its YOUR Turn To Be "Creator"!
Put YOUR Thoughts Here, and Read Them Later!

Now Its YOUR Turn To Be "Creator"!
Put YOUR Thoughts Here, and Read Them Later!

Now Its YOUR Turn To Be "Creator"!
Put YOUR Thoughts Here, and Read Them Later!

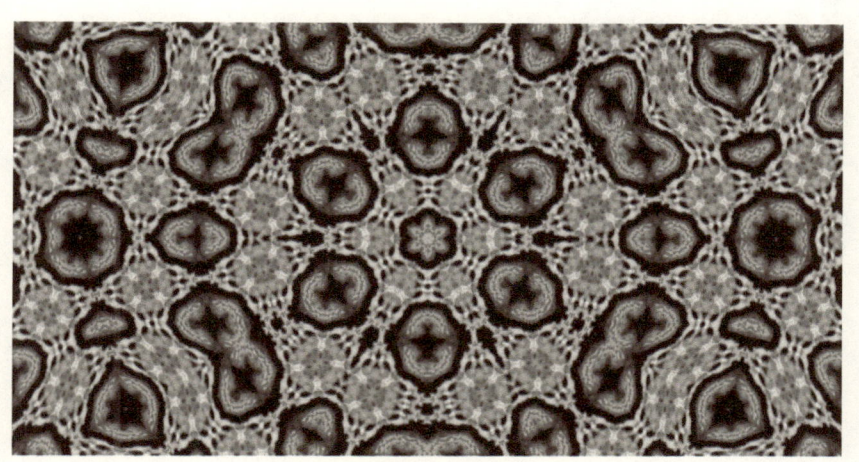

One Great Gift

www.pacepublishing.com

"One Great Gift"
Inspirational Background

Sometimes it is a cataclysmic event that dramatically alters the course of our lives, and sets us upon a path that leads directly into the fulfillment of our life's purpose; but at other times our leading is much more gentle, and subtle, and requires us to make some rather brave and daring decisions, ..., ones that the cataclysmic scenario would have seemingly imposed on us. It's hard to make choices when we still have so many choices to choose from! We work hard to get to where we are. We've expended a lot of energy, studied and developed a lot of skill's, and all of these have established us with a certain reputation among our peers, ..., a comfortable image of ourselves, and a recognized "position" that is not easily given up. We are comfortable in the perceived security of our job and it's adequate paycheck. We are attached to our humble abode (some more "humble" than others!) And, we have our familiar circle of friends and family to support us.

But, is that really all there is to life? What about those deep longings for something else that we keep *pushing aside? What about those inner dissatisfactions that we keep ignoring? After all, we're "established",..., "secure",..., and surrounded by symbols of "success". Why should we discomfit ourselves, let go of those things that we perceive as "guarantees" in our lives, and venture out into uncharted waters just because there seems to be an undefinable itch that we can't seem to scratch in our lives?*

*But, what if we could scratch that itch (if we only had the courage)? What if there really was an unrecognized acre of diamonds in our own backyard? What if there really was a "Master Plan" for your life? And, what if there really was **"One Great Gift"** that had been placed in you from the beginning, ..., that was unique to just you, ..., and would truly make your eyes light up (as it suggests in the following poem), ..., if you just had the courage to venture out and **DO IT** ? I challenge you to honestly admit to your self and to others what your unique gifting is, and then to pursue it with all diligence. It has a definite purpose for you, and for the universe at large! The world is waiting for your shiny piece to complete the giant "Kaleidoscope" of life!*

We are grateful to Dr. Wayne Dyer, who used his unique giftings to bring to international attention the remarkable story of the gracious heroine that we consider next.

Anita Moorjani (http://www.anitamoorjani.com/) is the author of "Dying To Be Me" (Hay House - published in 34 languages). I was first introduced to her through an Internet video that I found through an article on the In5d.com website (http://www.bodymindsoulspirit.com/this-womans-near-death-experience-will-change-your-pespective-about-everything/).

And their title was quite right! Her story is that she has been to the "other side" and has brought some very important, nay, critical lessons back to us that will help us live more meaningful lives. They're familiar guidelines, but sometimes we need a little reminder to do everything in Love, live Life fearlessly, laugh lots, reverence Life as a gift, and always be yourself, along with these quotes:

"We are all expressions of the same consciousness."

"Every person serves a purpose."

"Be fearless about being who you are."

"Embrace your uniqueness."

"Your only purpose is to find out who you are."

These were not the easily pushed aside admonitions from an unknowable historical figure who had lived in different times, and, therefore, could not possibly understand the problems and pressures of today's complex world. She was a real, flesh and blood **miracle** *standing before an awed and respectful crowd of her contemporaries, who were deeply appreciative of a message that rang somewhere down deep inside as a familiar truth.*

She was serenely and confidently sharing her story of, not just survival of a dread life-threatening disease, but of her **triumph** *over it, and the Life lessons* that she had learned as a result of it. She had been places that others of us had not been. She had seen the "other side", and come back, and she had been given to understand its workings as only one with experience could comprehend.

It was not something that she'd read in a book, but rather, she had actually let go of her life on this side of the veil, and was privileged to see how this thing we call Life functions in another dimension. From that perspective she could see her life and its true purpose here on earth with great clarity and understanding. She has come back to us with a challenging and encouraging message to live, love, laugh, and get on with the business of fearlessly **BEING** who We really **are**!

There is nothing new under the sun. Hers is an old message that deep down inside we have always known and understood. We knew it when we were children. We embodied it when we landed at the spaceport of our birthing room, but somehow in the entry processing through our Earthly Customs Office we have had our original cosmic hard drives overwritten with layer after layer of fear laden gobbledygook that pretty successfully hid the awesome, magnificent, and powerful force of energy that we really are.

And so, we have written a new program on our hard drives that maps to another set of emotions that were not included in the original design! It seems that the travel documents explaining the purpose of our trip somehow got misplaced. It is as if we have lost our cell phones that held all the contact numbers that gave us access to the universal energy that we came here to wield!. ET can't call home because we seem to have lost our connection!

And the result of this disconnect for many of us has been humdrum lives of quiet desperation, with a great absence of kick-up-your-heels joy, and a gnawing insidious grief smoldering somewhere inside of us that natters something about our failures to live up to some undefined expectations. Its the "downer" interpretation of the old hit song "Is That All There Is?" that we were discussing earlier in this book in the poem"**Where Am I?**".

But deep within each of us, as a part of our original equipment, lies a great unique passion, which, if awakened, and pursued with great diligence, will catapult our life into heights of great joy and accomplishment. Dedication to that passion is the key to the fulfillment of our purpose on earth. The accomplishment of bringing that assignment to completion will lead to great personal growth, radiant health on all levels of our existence, and rewards which will both elevate and deepen all aspects of our life.

Yes, there's something very unique that defines the real life purpose of each of us; something that really excites us and draws us; something that would give us a reason to be; in the pursuit of which we will fully develop the strengths and promises that are innate in all of us. Yes, the price of the emotional, physical, and mental demands may be overwhelming, but once the path is decisively set, and we are committed to the fulfillment of that perfectly tailored life's purpose here on earth, we will always find the resources that we laid up for the task flowing to us exactly on schedule. It will be a life filled with adventure, fulfillment, and a bit of the miraculous to add to our joy!

*Let me think now, ..., I'm unique, and its okay! I gotta give up my fears! Its actually **required** of me to love and value myself! I'm not a mistake. ... There really is a purpose for my life! I'm gonna hafta' work like crazy, but I can expect help and provision to do it! And, there's gonna be some rewards!*

***Yahoo! We can do this!** I feel a poem coming on!!!*

Poem
One Great Gift

What were You to be
    When You planned,
        And made **The Key**
        To your Life
            That You had planned
                From the beginning?

What was in Your Mind
    When The Plan You All designed
        Made You
            "One of a kind,"
                And Life worth living?

Whatever did You see
    Looking through
        Eternity,
            When You saw
                Ahead in time
                    To where You'd be?

Did You see You <u>where you are</u>?
 Or have Your footsteps
  Journeyed far
   From **The Plan**
    The Real I AM
     Had longed to see?

It was **Love's Amazing Grace**
 That put that look
  Upon your face
   And made the frame
    That is the strength
     For You to stand.

And then You saw
 Just where You'd fit;
  And how Your Life would benefit
   Through **One Great Gift**
    That has been placed
     Within Your hand.

That **"One Great Gift"**
    That brings you **Joy**
        More than any childhood toy
            That was fashioned
                From the Earth,
                    For man to see.

That **"One Great Gift"**
    That was devised
        That puts a sparkle in Your eyes
            That is the Spring
                From which will flow
                    All **You** can **BE!**

CHORUS

One Great Gift

That puts a smile upon Your face!

One Great Gift

That makes the world a better place!

One Great Gift

That was designed for **you to be!**

That

    One

        Great

            Gift

                We put

                    IN

                        ME!!!!!

TAG

Lift up Your Voice and start to Sing
    And let the rafters **really ring!**

When You have found that pearl of price
    That's worth a Life of sacrifice!!!

Then Life has purpose, and You'll see

What's truly meant
    For You TO BE!!!!!

                              2005 Vanessa Conaway Pace
                      Seattle, Washington, September 29, 2005

Song

One Great Gift
What Were You To Be?

Vanessa Conaway Pace

Vanessa Conaway Pace

(A Gift in Me!!! For all to see!

Let there be "One Great Gift" that puts a smile up-on Your face! "One Great Gift" that makes the world a bet-ter

2005

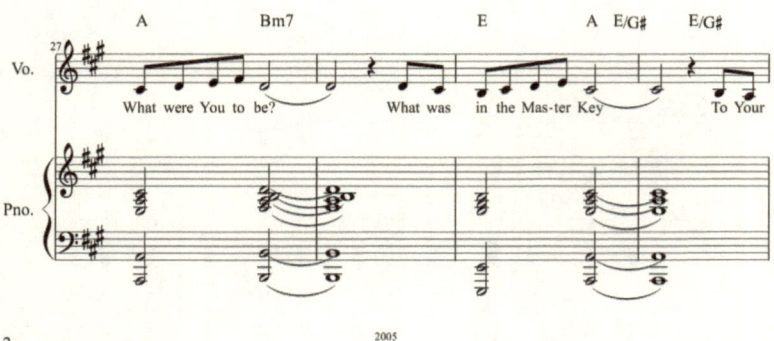

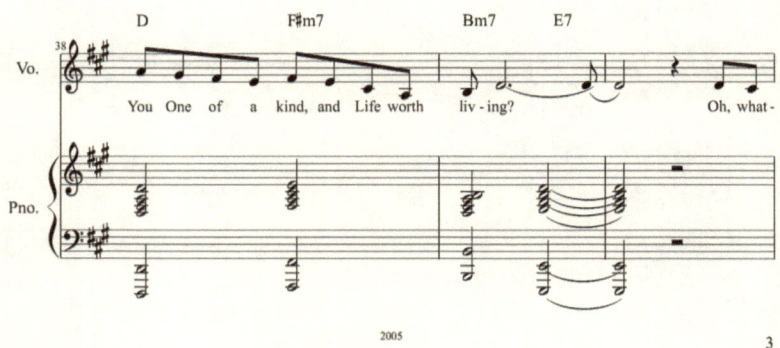

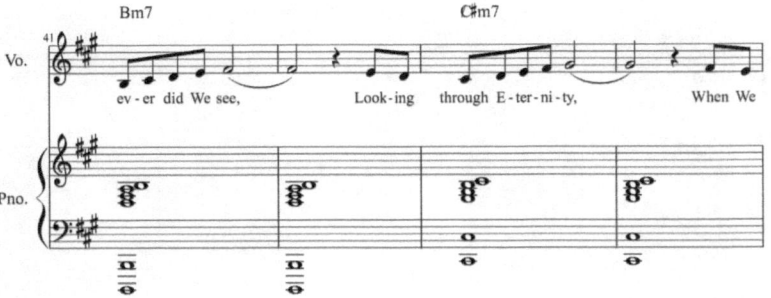
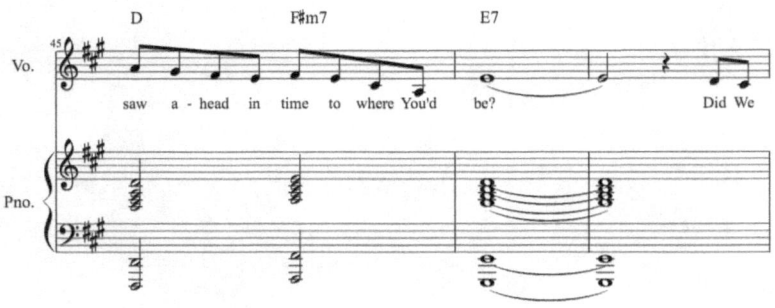
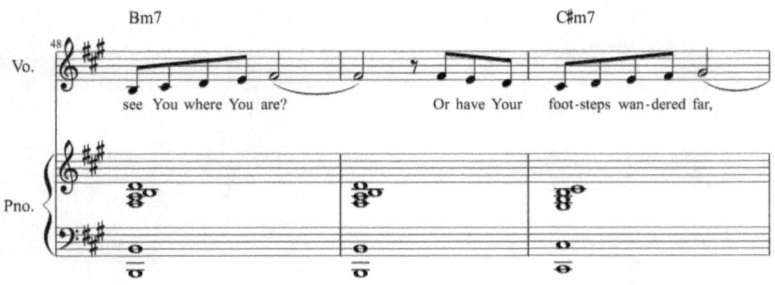

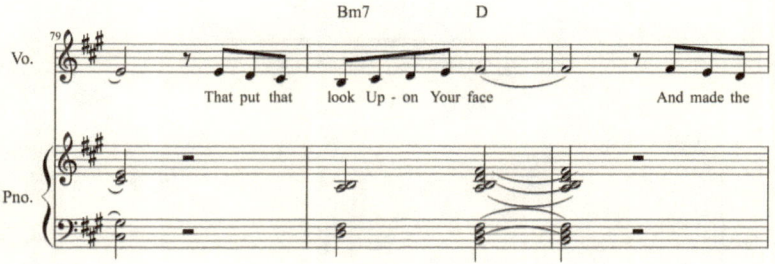

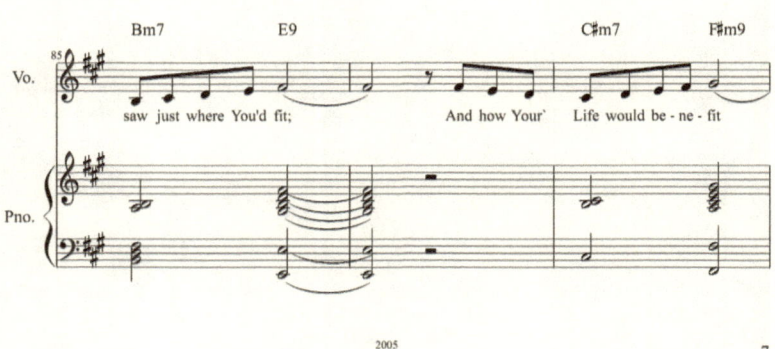

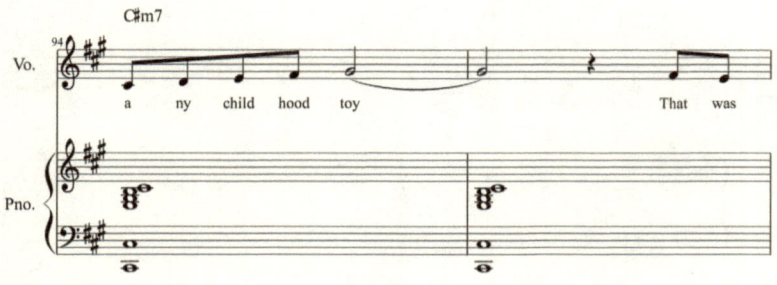

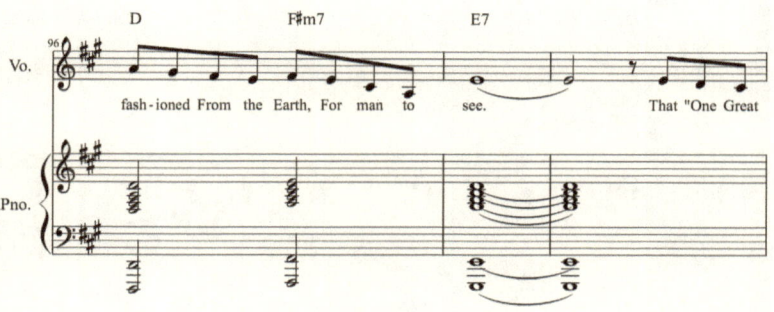

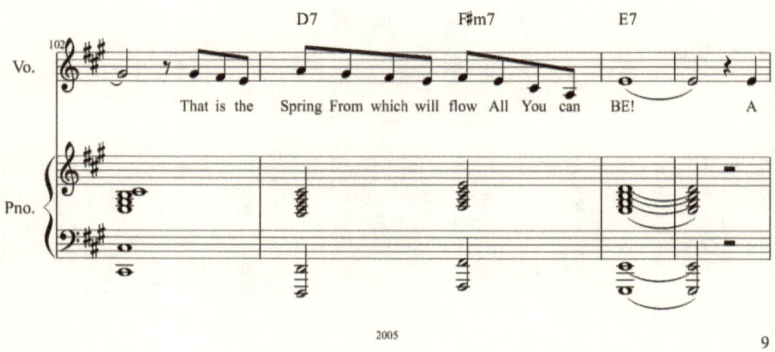

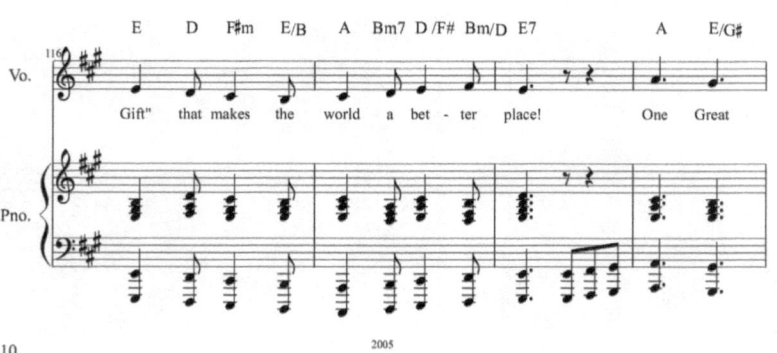

One Great Gift

This Is Your Invitation To Create!

Dear Seeker of Those "Deeper Things",

You know
    You have a talent,
        And a Gift
           That lies Within,
              But the problem is, …,
                  It's hard to to find
                  The place
                      We can begin

To share the wealth
    We've sheltered
        While We've lived
           The rest of Life,
              With its ups and downs,
                  It's win and lose,
                      It's good times,
                          And its strife;.

But that **One Gift**
    That's bubbling there,
        That You've held
           Like a miser,
              Is just about
                  To blow its hole,
                      And come up
                          Like a geyser!

So, give it shape,
    And write it down, …,
        …, **You** choose where it is going,
        And when you've finally
           Finished it
                You'll be the one
                      Who's crowing!!!

Now Its YOUR Turn To Be "Creator"!
Put YOUR Thoughts Here, and Read Them Later!

Now that You're thinking
    Of all that You ARE,
        Get out Your Book,
            And keep yourself
                On par!

Now Its YOUR Turn To Be "Creator"!
Put YOUR Thoughts Here, and Read Them Later!

Now Its YOUR Turn To Be "Creator"!
Put YOUR Thoughts Here, and Read Them Later!

*Now Its YOUR Turn To Be "Creator"!
Put YOUR Thoughts Here, and Read Them Later!*

Epilogue

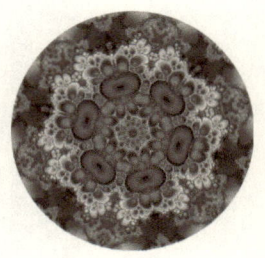

www.pacepublishing.com

Epilogue

Come,
    Sit in the sun,
        Or share the shade,
           And realize
        We've got it made!

    We landed here,
        Expenses paid,
           To help pull off
              Earth's new upgrade!

  We never thought
      We couldn't do it,
         Or, that our minds
            Could not intuit

    How this system
        Really works, ...,
           We're just a bunch
              Of Captain Kirks!!!

Together,
    We can do it all!!
        There is
           No big part,
              And, no small,

        Its just
           That each
              Must heed the call
                  That's been sent out
                      To one and all!

To make this world
    A better place,
        And to get your self
            Back in the race
                By dusting off
                    The dream inside
                        And giving it
                            A Joyous ride.

'Cause You
    No longer
        Have to hide
            That longing
                That you feared
                    Had died.

In this new day
    You have a chance
        To make your dream
            Stand up
                And dance!

You really **can**
    Kick up Your heels,
        And know how Freedom
            Really feels! ...!

It only takes
    A strong Decision,
        That's executed
            With concision,
                And then
                    Just don't allow
                        Division,
                          Or anyone
                            To cast
                              Derision.....

Just set
>	Your dream
>>		In front of you,
>>>			And then
>>>>				You'll know
>>>>>					Just what
>>>>>>						To do....

Ideas will come, ...,
>	Provisions, too! ...!
>>		And you
>>>			Will have
>>>>				A Dream
>>>>>					Come true!

And You
>	Will know
>>		The satisfaction
>>>			That comes
>>>>				From simply
>>>>>					Taking action!

Forget the Can'ts,
>	And Won'ts,
>>		And Fears
>>>			That have had
>>>>				You stuck
>>>>>					For all
>>>>>>						These years,
>	Then step right up,
>>		And face the plate,
>>>			**And knock the ball**
>>>>				**Clean through**
>>>>>					**The gate!!!**

And **do** the thing
    That makes you happy, ...,
        Just step right up,
            And make it snappy; ...;
    Collect your tools
        And your ideas
           And work
                Like that Great
                    Herculeas

    Until You've conquered
        All your mountains
           And opened those
                Creative fountains!!!

So, stretch your wings
    And start to fly, ...,
        You'll find that you
           Will cease to cry
                About the things
                    You might have done,

            (**That** sure leaves
                Your life
                    Undone!)

    But, now
        You're having
            Lots of fun, ...
                And empty days
                    Are on the run.

So, ..., rise up
    To this great
        Occasion,
            And join
                This "Cre-a-tive"
                    Invasion
    That's bringing
        New Life
            To the Earth.
            Please,
                Do **your** part
                    To give it birth!

We've learned,
    And grown
        In Volume Two
            And maybe
                Thought some new things
                    Through;
And now,
    We're on
        To Volume Three!!!
            Where more adventures
                Wait for Thee!!!
So, Grab your pen,
    And settle in,
        And *let*
            Your NEW
                EPOCH
                    BEGIN!!!

                            Vanessa Conaway Pace
                Lynnwood, Washington, February 24, 2015

www.pacepublishing.com

Epilogue

This Is Your Invitation To Create!

Dear Seeker of Those "Deeper Things",

Its Your turn now
      To show your stuff,
           And even if
                The going's tough

    The seed
        Is there
          Inside
              Of YOU

      Of what
          You came
              To Earth
                  To do!!

So, plant it
    With some
        Loving care

        And tend it
           Like a good
                Au pair;

And soon
      You'll grow
         A crop
            So splendid

        That all
           Will know
              It was
                Intended!!!

Now Its YOUR Turn To Be "Creator"!
Put YOUR Thoughts Here, and Read Them Later!

Continue with
    The Book
        You've started,
            And write
                The ideas
                    We've imparted!

*Now Its YOUR Turn To Be "Creator"!
Put YOUR Thoughts Here, and Read Them Later!*

Now Its YOUR Turn To Be "Creator"!
Put YOUR Thoughts Here, and Read Them Later!

*Now Its YOUR Turn To Be "Creator"!
Put YOUR Thoughts Here, and Read Them Later!*

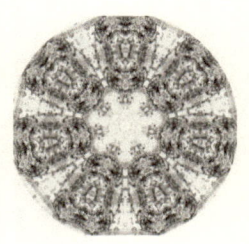

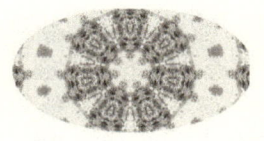

Reading List

www.pacepublishing.com

Reading List

TITLE	AUTHOR	PUBLISHER	LOCATION
Awaken To The Healer Within	Rich Work	Asini Publishing	Mosinee, WI
Brain Magic	Neil Slade	Neil Slade Music and Books	Denver, CO
Chariots of the Gods	Erich Von Daniken	Bantam Books	New York, NY
Color and Music in the New Age	Corinne Heline	Devorss and Company, Publishers	Marina del Rey, CA
Color Healing: Chromotherapy and How It Works	Mary Anderson	The Aquarian Press	Wellingborough, Northamptonshire, England
Communing with Music	Matthew Cantello	DeVorss & Company	Camarillo, CA
Cosmic Conversations	Neil Slade	Neil Slade Music and Books	Denver, CO

TITLE	AUTHOR	PUBLISHER	LOCATION
Do What You Love, The Money Will Follow	Marsha Sinetar	Dell Publishing division of Bantam Doubleday	New York, NY
Embraced by The Light	Betty J. Eadie	Gold Leaf Press	Placerville, CA
Energy Medicine	Donna Eden	Jeremy P. Tarcher/Putnam, a member of Penguin Putnam Inc.	New York, NY
Finding Water: The Art of Perseverance	Julia Cameron	Jeremy P. Tarcher/Penguin, a member of Penguin Group (USA) Inc.	New York, NY
Gods from Outer Space	Erich Von Daniken	Bantam Books	New York, NY
Harmonograph: A Visualn Guide To the Mathematics of Music	Anthony Ashton	Walker & Company	New York, NY

TITLE	AUTHOR	PUBLISHER	LOCATION
Healing At The Speed of Sound	Don Campbell and Alex Doman	Hudson Street Press, Penguin Group (USA) Inc.	New York, NY
Healing Sounds	Jonathan Goldman		
In Search of Ancient Gods	Erich Von Daniken	Bantam Books	New York, NY
Music Forms	Geoffrey Hodson	The Theosophical Publishing House	Adyar, Chennai 600 020, India; Wheaton, IL
Secret Sounds, Ultimate Healing	Jill Mattson	Wings of Light	Oil City, PA
The Chakras and the Human Energy Fields	Shafica Karagulla, M.D. and Dora van Gelder Kunz	The Theosophical Publishing House	Wheaton, IL, USA; Madras, India; London, England
The Cosmic Octave: Origin of Harmony; Planets-Tones-Colors-The Power of Inherent Vibrations (Harmonic Concert Pitch)	Hans Cousto	Life Rhythm Publication	Mendocino, CA

TITLE	AUTHOR	PUBLISHER	LOCATION
The Emotion Code	Dr. Bradley Nelson	Wellness Unmasked Publishing	Mesquite, NV
The Force	Stuart Wilde	Wisdom Books, Inc.	Taos, NM
The God of the Gods	Erich Von Daniken	Bantam Books	New York
The Healer's Manual: A Beginner's Guide to Energy Therapies	Ted Andrews	Llewellyn Publications	St. Paul, MN
The Healing Power of Water	Dr. Masuro Emoto	Hay House, Inc.	Carlsbad, CA
The Healing Voice	Joy Gardner-Gordon	The Crossing Press	Freedom, CA
The Kingdom of the Gods	Geoffrey Hodson	The Theosophical Publishing House	Adyar, Chennai 600 020, India; Wheaton, IL, USA
The Roar of Silence: Healing Powers of Breath, Tone & Music	Don G. Campbell	The Theosophical Publishing House	Wheaton, Ill., USA; Madras, India; London, England

Request for Reader's Review

There's a "Poet"
    That's living
        On the inside
           Of YOU!!!

And Its speaking
    For The One
        That lives in Me
           TOO!

Hoping You
    Have enjoyed
        All these Books
           Through and through,

And that You'd
    Be so kind
        As to write
           A Review!!!

And to post it
>   To Amazon's
>   Page for this Book
>   So that others
>   Will know
>   To give THIS BOOK
>   A LOOK!!!

And maybe
>   You'll send it
>   To this "Poet"
>   TOO!

So I can say
>   "Thank You"
>   For seeing that
>   Through!!!

This Poet, and The Poetry Muses will Thank You!!!

For
> Concerts that make
>> You Laugh and Cry,

> Creative products
>> That You'll want to buy,

> Poetry that makes
>> You see new things,

> And Wisdom on Voice
>> That'll help You Sing!

Contact Vanessa Pace at
> www.pacepublishing.com
>> Post Office Box 2187, Lynnwood, WA 98036

www.pacepublishing.com

www.pacepublishing.com

www.ingramcontent.com/pod-product-compliance
Lightning Source LLC
Chambersburg PA
CBHW030436300426
44112CB00009B/1031